CliffsNo

Wuthering Heights

By Richard Wasowski, M.A.

IN THIS BOOK

- Learn about the Life and Background of the Author
- Preview an Introduction to the Novel
- Explore themes, character development, and recurring images in the Critical Commentaries
- Examine an in-depth Character Analysis
- Acquire an understanding of the novel with Critical Essays
- Reinforce what you learn with CliffsNotes Review
- Find additional information to further your study in the CliffsNotes Resource Center and online at www.cliffsnotes.com

WILEY

Wiley Publishing, Inc.

About the Author

Richard Wasowski earned his M.A. from The Ohio State University and teaches secondary English in Ashland, Ohio.

Composition

Indexer: York Production Services, Inc.
Proofreader: York Production Services, Inc.
Wiley Indianapolis Composition Services

Publisher's Acknowledgments

Editorial

Project Editor: Tere Drenth
Acquisitions Editor: Gregory W. Tubach
Glossary Editors: The editors and staff of Webster's New World Dictionary
Editorial Administrator: Michelle Hacker

CliffsNotes™ *Wuthering Heights*

Published by:
Wiley Publishing, Inc.
111 River Street
Hoboken, NJ 07030
www.wiley.com

Library of Congress Cataloging-in-Publication Data
Wasowski, Richard.
    Cliff Notes, Wuthering Heights /
by Richard Wasowski.
        p.   cm.
    Includes bibliographical references and index.
    ISBN 978-0-7645-8594-4 (alk. paper)
    1. Brontë, Emily, 1818-1848. Wuthering Heights--Examinations--Study guides I. Title: Wuthering Heights. II. Title
PR4172.W73 W37 2000
823'.8--dc21   00–035081
                                                              CIP

Table of Contents

How to Use This Book

This CliffsNotes study guide on Emily Bronte's *Wuthering Heights* supplements the original literary work, giving you background information about the author, an introduction to the work, a graphical character map, critical commentaries, expanded glossaries, and a comprehensive index, all for you to use as an educational tool that will allow you to better understand *Wuthering Heights.* This study guide was written with the assumption that you have read *Wuthering Heights.* Reading a literary work doesn't mean that you immediately grasp the major themes and devices used by the author; this study guide will help supplement your reading to be sure you get all you can from Emily bronte's *Wuthering Heights.* CliffsNotes Review tests your comprehension of the original text and reinforces learning with questions and answers, practice projects, and more. For further information on Emily Bronte and *Wuthering Heights,* check out the CliffsNotes Resource Center.

CliffsNotes provides the following icons to highlight essential elements of particular interest:

Reveals the underlying themes in the work.

Helps you to more easily relate to or discover the depth of a character.

Uncovers elements such as setting, atmosphere, mystery, passion, violence, irony, symbolism, tragedy, foreshadowing, and satire.

Enables you to appreciate the nuances of words and phrases.

Don't Miss Our Web Site

Discover classic literature as well as modern-day treasures by visiting the Cliffs Notes Web site at www.cliffsnotes.com. You can obtain a quick download of a CliffsNotes title, purchase a title in print form, browse our catalog, or view online samples.

LIFE AND BACKGROUND OF THE AUTHOR

The following abbreviated biography of Emily Bronte is provided so that you might become more familiar with her life and the historical times that possibly influenced her writing. Read this Life and Background of the Author section and recall it when reading Bronte's *Wuthering Heights,* thinking of any thematic relationship between Bronte's novel and her life.

Personal Background

"*Wuthering Heights* is a strange sort of book—baffling all regular criticism; yet, it is impossible to begin and not finish it; and quite as impossible to lay it aside afterwards and say nothing about it." This review, from *Douglas Jerrold's Weekly Newspaper*, was one of the first receptions to Emily Brontë's novel, and concluded with the line, "we must leave it to our readers to decide what sort of a book it is." The conclusion in this review, which is the extent of praise the novel received on its publication, pertains not only to the novel *Wuthering Heights* but to Emily Brontë herself; it is up to readers to determine what type of writer Brontë was: Besides *Wuthering Heights*, only a few poems of hers exist and precious little of her personal history exists to complement those writings. Thus, in order to ascertain what type of writer Brontë was, critics must speculate based on a limited family history, some poems, and one excellent novel.

Brontë was one of six children born to Reverend Patrick Brontë and Maria Branwell Brontë. Born in Thornton, Yorkshire, England, on July 30, 1818, she was the sister of Maria, Elizabeth, Charlotte, Anne, and Branwell. Her family moved to Haworth when she was two years old, and here she first experienced the moors, a part of the Pennine Chain of mountains, andhere she lived until she died 30 years later.

A variety of conflicting influences shaped her life. Her father, of Irish descent, was known for his poetry and imagination even though he was the cleric. Her mother, a staunch Methodist, died when Emily was only three years old, so what she knew of her she learned from her siblings and her Aunt Elizabeth (Maria's sister), who raised the children after Maria's death. Elizabeth brought a religious fervor to the house that Brontë soon rejected.

Brontë's environment shaped her life and her work. The village of Haworth was isolated and surrounded by moors; thus, the one world she knew and lived in became the setting for her only novel. Paralleling her own life, she creates motherless characters in *Wuthering Heights*.

Writing was a means of amusement for the Brontë children. After the two oldest sisters died, the remaining siblings began writing plays and poems, creating a world called Angria and Gondal. These worlds became little books and the sources for later poetry and prose. Emily Brontë went to school, but she was unable to stay there. Possessing a reclusive nature, she had longings and desires for her home on the moors, which prompted her return home after a scant three months.

In the following year, 1837, she attempted to teach school. This endeavor lasted eight months, but she could not handle the stress and again returned home. In 1842 she went with Charlotte to Brussels to study foreign languages and school management in order to open a school in Haworth. Brontë had success there. One of her professors stated that she "had a head for logic and a capability for argument, unusual in a man, and rare indeed in a woman," but she returned to Haworth when her aunt died in 1843. Living with her father at the parsonage in Haworth, this became a period of creativity. Although the earliest dated poem is from 1836, the majority of her poetry that survives was written during this time.

Career Highlights

Like most authors, Emily Brontë was a product of her environment, and this directly influenced her writing. During her life she had no close friends, was interested in mysticism, and enjoyed her solitude outdoors. All of these elements grace both her poems and *Wuthering Heights*. In fact, many contemporary critics praise Emily Brontë first and foremost as a poet, marveling at the poetic nature of *Wuthering Heights*.

In 1845 Charlotte found some of the poetry that Emily had been writing and eventually persuaded her sister to attempt to publish her work. Charlotte and Emily, along with their sister Anne, eventually published a collection of poems under the male names of Currer, Ellis, and Acton Bell. Each pseudonym begins with the same consonant as the writer's name. The sisters paid to have the collection published, and even though it only sold two copies, they were undaunted and continued to write. This time each sister wrote a novel.

Evidence suggests that Emily Brontë began writing *Wuthering Heights* in December 1845 and completed it the next year. A year after that, in July of 1847, *Wuthering Heights* was accepted for publication; however, it was not printed until December, following the success of *Jane Eyre*.

Although *Wuthering Heights* did not meet with the critical success *Jane Eyre* received, contemporary critics tend to consider Emily the best writer of the Brontë sisters. Emily Brontë's highly imaginative novel of passion and hate was too savage and animal-like and clumsy in its own day and time, but contemporary audiences consider it mild.

The fall following publication, Emily Brontë left home to attend her brother's funeral. She caught a severe cold that spread to her lungs, and she died of tuberculosis on December 19, 1848.

Following the publication of poems, *Jane Eyre*, *Wuthering Heights*, and Anne's novel *Agnes Grey*, audiences considered all three "Bells" to be one author. Confusion continued as Anne published *The Tenant of Wildfell Hall*. *Wuthering Heights* was reissued with poems and a biographical notice by Charlotte. By this time, both Emily and Anne had died, and Charlotte succinctly stated how and why she and her sisters assumed the name of Bell. Charlotte Brontë also provided insight into the life of her sister.

Long after its initial publication and subsequent death of its author, *Wuthering Heights* has become one of the classics of English literature. After the reissue of Emily Brontë's text, the editors of the *Examiner* commented upon Charlotte's introduction. Their words and sentiments are often echoed by admirers of *Wuthering Heights*: "We have only most unfeignedly to deplore the blight which fell prematurely on sure rich intellectual promise, and to regret that natures so rare and noble should so early have passed away."

INTRODUCTION TO THE NOVEL

The following Introduction section is provided solely as an educational tool and is not meant to replace the experience of your reading the novel. Read the Introduction and A Brief Synopsis to enhance your understanding of the novel and to prepare yourself for the critical thinking that should take place whenever you read any work of fiction or nonfiction. Keep the List of Characters and Character Map at hand so that as you read the original literary work, if you encounter a character about whom you're uncertain, you can refer to the List of Characters and Character Map to refresh your memory.

Introduction

Although *Wuthering Heights* received neither critical praise nor any local popularity during its initial publication, the reading public has changed substantially since 1847, and now both critical and popular opinion praise Emily Brontë's singular work of fiction. Victorian society would not accept the violent characters and harsh realities of *Wuthering Heights*, but subsequent audiences are both more understanding and accepting of the use of unsavory aspects of human life in literature.

The first person to praise publicly *Wuthering Heights* was Charlotte Brontë, Emily's sister, who wrote a preface and introduction for the second publication of the novel in 1850 and became the novel's first and foremost critic. Yet Charlotte herself was not entirely convinced of all its merits. Commenting upon the advisability of creating characters such as Heathcliff, Charlotte states, "I scarcely think it is [advisable]." Charlotte's comments may be a direct concession and appeal to Victorian audiences to accept and respect *Wuthering Heights* without having to accept completely everything within the text. In addition to having difficulty with the content, the Victorian audience's view of women could not allow anyone of that period to accept that *Wuthering Heights* was the creation of a female (it had been published originally under the pseudonym Ellis Bell). After its initial publication, both critical and popular audiences ended up embracing *Wuthering Heights*, and it remains one of the classic works still read and studied.

Wuthering Heights is an important contemporary novel for two reasons: Its honest and accurate portrayal of life during an early era provides a glimpse of history, and the literary merit it possesses in and of itself enables the text to rise above entertainment and rank as quality literature. The portrayal of women, society, and class bear witness to a time that's foreign to contemporary readers. But even though society is different today than it was two centuries ago, people remain the same, and contemporary readers can still relate to the feelings and emotions of the central characters—Heathcliff and Catherine—as well as those of the supporting characters. Because Brontë's characters are real, they are human subjects with human emotions; therefore, *Wuthering Heights* is not just a sentimental romance novel. It is a presentation of life, an essay on love, and a glimpse at relationships. Many critics, praising Brontë's style, imagery, and word choice, contend that *Wuthering Heights* is actually poetry masquerading as prose.

This lyrical prose has a distinct structure and style. Significantly, *Wuthering Heights* is about ordered pairs: two households, two generations, and two pairs of children. Some critics dismiss the plot of the second-generation characters as being a simple retelling of the first story; however, in doing so, they are dismissing the entire second half of the book. Each of the two main story lines of the two generations comprises 17 chapters. Clearly, in order to appreciate fully *Wuthering Heights*, attention must be paid to the second half, particularly noting that the second half is not just a retelling but rather a revising—a form of renewal and rebirth.

These ordered pairs more often than not, are pairs of contrast. The most noticeable pair is that of the two houses: Wuthering Heights and Thrushcross Grange. Wuthering Heights has the wild, windy moors and its inhabitants possess the same characteristics. Opposite this are the calm, orderly parks of Thrushcross Grange and its inhabitants. Each household has a male and female with a counterpart at the other. Readers gain insight into these characters not only by observing what they think, say, and do but also by comparing them to their counterparts, noticing how they do not think, speak, and act. Much is learned by recognizing what one is not.

Structurally, the narrative is also primarily told from a paired point of view. Lockwood frames the initial story, telling the beginning and ending chapters (with minor comments within). Within the framework of his story, Nelly relates the majority of the action from her outsider's point of view. In essence, readers are eavesdropping rather than experiencing the action. And embedded within Nelly's narrative are chapters told primarily from another character's point of view that has been related to Nelly. This technique allows readers to experience more than would with any one narrator, enabling readers to gain an insider's perspective.

The role of the outsider should not be overlooked because the setting of *Wuthering Heights* is one of complete isolation; therefore, only those with first- or second-hand experiences are able to relate them to others. The moors connecting Wuthering Heights and Thrushcross Grange serve a dual purpose—linking the two households while simultaneously separating them from the village and all others.

This isolated setting is important for Brontë's combination of realism and gothic symbolism. Brontë took conventions of the time and instead of merely recreating them in a work of her own, used them as a springboard to write an entirely original tale, creating characters who are simultaneously real and symbolic archetypes.

Brontë uses these characters to explore themes of good versus evil, crime and punishment, passion versus rationality, revenge, selfishness, division and reconciliation, chaos and order, nature and culture, health and sickness, rebellion, and the nature of love. These themes are not independent of each other; rather, they mix, mingle, and intertwine as the story unfolds.

Wuthering Heights is also a social novel about class structure in society as well as a treatise on the role of women. Brontë illustrates how class mobility is not always moving in one direction. For Catherine, representing a lower class, social class plays a major role when deciding to get married. That is why she cannot marry Heathcliff and agrees, instead, to marry Edgar. For Isabella, however, just the opposite is true. She is drawn to the wild, mysterious man, regardless of the fact that he is beneath her social standing. Because of her infatuation, she loses everything that is dear to her. Readers must therefore look not only to social class when judging and analyzing characters; they must determine what decisions are made by members of a certain class and why these characters made the decisions they did.

On the surface, *Wuthering Heights* is a love story. Delving deeper, readers find both a symbolic and psychological novel. (Contemporary audiences, for example, easily relate to issues of child abuse and alcoholism.) In fact, *Wuthering Heights* cannot be easily classified as any particular type of novel—that is the literary strength that Brontë's text possesses. The novel told from multiple points of view is easily read and interpreted from multiple perspectives, also.

Like other literary masterpieces, *Wuthering Heights* has spawned dramatic productions, a musical retelling, movies, and even a novel that fills in the gaps of Heathcliff's three missing years. Emily Brontë's novel has overcome its initial chilly reception to warm the hearts of romantics and realists worldwide.

A Brief Synopsis

Wuthering Heights opens with Lockwood, a tenant of Heathcliff's, visiting the home of his landlord. A subsequent visit to Wuthering Heights yields an accident and a curious supernatural encounter, which pique Lockwood's curiosity. Back at Thrushcross Grange and recuperating from his illness, Lockwood begs Nelly Dean, a servant who grew up in Wuthering Heights and now cares for Thrushcross Grange, to tell him of the history of Heathcliff. Nelly narrates the main plot line of *Wuthering Heights*.

Mr. Earnshaw, a Yorkshire Farmer and owner of Wuthering Heights, brings home an orphan from Liverpool. The boy is named Heathcliff and is raised with the Earnshaw children, Hindley and Catherine. Catherine loves Heathcliff but Hindley hates him because Heathcliff has replaced Hindley in Mr. Earnshaw's affection. After Mr. Earnshaw's death, Hindley does what he can to destroy Heathcliff, but Catherine and Heathcliff grow up playing wildly on the moors, oblivious of anything or anyone else—until they encounter the Lintons.

Edgar and Isabella Linton live at Thrushcross Grange and are the complete opposites of Heathcliff and Catherine. The Lintons welcome Catherine into their home but shun Heathcliff. Treated as an outsider once again, Heathcliff begins to think about revenge. Catherine, at first, splits her time between Heathcliff and Edgar, but soon she spends more time with Edgar, which makes Heathcliff jealous. When Heathcliff overhears Catherine tell Nelly that she can never marry him (Heathcliff), he leaves Wuthering Heights and is gone for three years.

While he is gone, Catherine continues to court and ends up marrying Edgar. Their happiness is short-lived because they are from two different worlds, and their relationship is strained further when Heathcliff returns. Relationships are complicated even more as Heathcliff winds up living with his enemy, Hindley (and Hindley's son, Hareton), at Wuthering Heights and marries Isabella, Edgar's sister. Soon after Heathcliff's marriage, Catherine gives birth to Edgar's daughter, Cathy, and dies.

Heathcliff vows revenge and does not care who he hurts while executing it. He desires to gain control of Wuthering Heights and Thrushcross Grange and to destroy everything Edgar Linton holds dear. In order to exact his revenge, Heathcliff must wait 17 years. Finally, he forces Cathy to marry his son, Linton. By this time he has control of the Heights and with Edgar's death, he has control of the Grange.

Through all of this, though, the ghost of Catherine haunts Heathcliff. What he truly desires more than anything else is to be reunited with his soul mate. At the end of the novel, Heathcliff and Catherine are united in death, and Hareton and Cathy are going to be united in marriage.

List of Characters

Heathcliff The main character. Orphaned as a child, he is constantly on the outside, constantly losing people. Although he and Catherine Earnshaw profess that they complete each other, her decision to marry Edgar Linton almost destroys their relationship. He spends most of his life contemplating and acting out revenge. He is abusive, brutal, and cruel.

Catherine Earnshaw The love of Heathcliff's life. Wild, impetuous, and arrogant as a child, she grows up getting everything she wants. When two men fall in love with her, she torments both of them. Ultimately, Catherine's selfishness ends up hurting everyone she loves, including herself.

Edgar Linton Catherine's husband and Heathcliff's rival. Well-mannered and well-to-do, he falls in love with and marries Catherine. His love for her enables him to overlook their incompatible natures.

Cathy Linton Daughter of Catherine and Edgar. A mild form of her mother, she serves as a reminder of her mother's strengths and weaknesses. (Note: For the purpose of clarity, the younger Catherine is referred to as "Cathy" in this Note, and her mother is referred to as "Catherine." This convention is not used in the original text.)

Linton Heathcliff Son of Heathcliff and Isabella. Weak and whiny (both physically and emotionally), he serves as a pawn in Heathcliff's game of revenge. He marries Cathy.

Hareton Earnshaw Catherine's nephew, son of Hindley. Although uneducated and unrefined, Hareton has a staunch sense of pride. He is attracted to Cathy but put off by her attitude. His generous heart enables the two of them to eventually fall in love and marry. Hareton is the only person to mourn Heathcliff's death.

Ellen (Nelly) Dean The primary narrator and Catherine's servant. Although she is one person capable of relating the majority of the events that occurred, she is not without bias.

Lockwood Heathcliff's tenant at Thrushcross Grange and the impetus for Nelly's narration. Although he serves primarily as the catalyst for the story, Lockwood's role is an outsider who happens to gain inside information. His visit to Wuthering Heights and subsequent actions directly affect the plot.

Mr. Earnshaw Catherine's father. He brings Heathcliff into his family and soon favors the orphan over his own son, Hindley.

Mrs. Earnshaw Catherine's mother. Not much is known about her, except that she favors her own son to Heathcliff, whom she does not like.

Hindley Earnshaw Catherine's brother. Jealous of Heathcliff, he takes a bit of revenge on Heathcliff after his father dies. He proves to be no match for Heathcliff, however, eventually losing his son and his family's home.

Frances Earnshaw Hindley's wife. A sickly woman who dies soon after Hareton is born.

Joseph Servant at Wuthering Heights. A hypocritical zealot who possesses a religious fanaticism that most find wearisome.

Mr. and Mrs. Linton Edgar's parents. They welcome Catherine into her home, introducing her to the life in upper society. They die soon after nursing Catherine back to health.

Isabella Edgar's sister. Her infatuation with Heathcliff causes her to destroy her relationship with her brother. She experiences Heathcliff's brutality first hand. She flees to London where she gives birth to Heathcliff's son, but her attempts to keep her son from his father fail.

Zillah Heathcliff's housekeeper. She saves Lockwood from a pack of dogs and serves as Nelly's source of information at Wuthering Heights.

Character Map

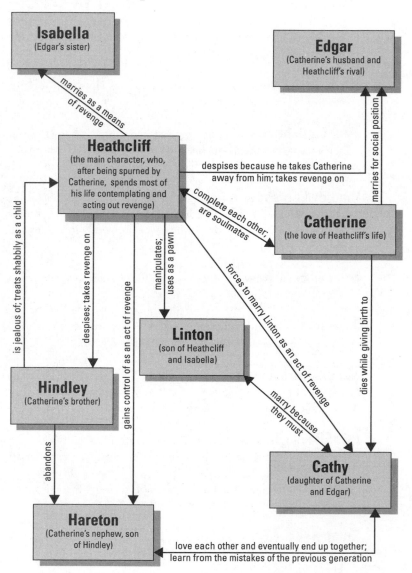

CRITICAL COMMENTARIES

The sections that follow provide great tools for supplementing your reading of *Wuthering Heights*. First, in order to enhance your understanding of and enjoyment from reading, we provide quick summaries in case you have difficulty when you read the original literary work. Each summary is followed by commentary: literary devices, character analyses, themes, and so on. Keep in mind that the interpretations here are solely those of the author of this study guide and are used to jumpstart your thinking about the work. No single interpretation of a complex work like *Wuthering Heights* is infallible or exhaustive, and you'll likely find that you interpret portions of the work differently from the author of this study guide. Read the original work and determine your own interpretations, referring to these Notes for supplemental meanings only.

Chapter 1

Summary

Wuthering Heights opens with Mr. Lockwood, a new tenant at Thrushcross Grange, writing in his diary about his visit to his landlord, Mr. Heathcliff. While entering Wuthering Heights, Lockwood notices but does not comment upon the date "1500" and the name "Hareton Earnshaw" above the principal door. Lockwood, an unwelcome guest, soon meets Joseph, a servant, and a pack of dogs that have overrun the farmhouse. Although he receives no encouragement from his host, Lockwood decides to make a return visit.

Commentary

Wuthering Heights opens with a date that signifies the setting as well as the form of the narrative. The present is 1801; however, the primary story line has taken place years ago. Most of the action in the novel occurs in Wuthering Heights, Thrushcross Grange, or the moors in between the two houses. All three locations are "completely removed from the stir of society," and each house symbolizes its habitants: Those at Wuthering Heights tend to be strong, wild, and passionate whereas those at Thrushcross Grange are passive, civilized, and calm. Heathcliff is the personification of Wuthering Heights.

Character Insight

Readers are introduced to Lockwood, an unreliable narrator who tries to make sense of his surroundings and his landlord. In doing so, his impressions provide readers with the first glimpse of Heathcliff, the main character. Lockwood's perceptions are simultaneously significant for the reader while being wholly inaccurate for himself as a character. For example, he mentions twice that Heathcliff does not extend a hand to him, yet Lockwood still considers Heathcliff a gentleman. Lockwood also notices that "grass grows up between the flags, and cattle are the only hedgecutters" but erroneously assumes that Heathcliff has a "whole establishment of domestics." At the close of the chapter, Lockwood recognizes that Heathcliff has no desire to see him again, yet he plans to visit again nonetheless. Lockwood draws comparisons between Heathcliff and himself, and the line "I have gained the reputation of deliberate heartlessness" foreshadows the telling of past heartless actions by Heathcliff.

Lockwood is clearly blind to the reality of the situation, although the extent of his misinterpretations is not fully realized. He is the first of many narrators to tell the story from a point of view that is neither omniscient nor unbiased. In *Wuthering Heights*, stories are often told within stories, with much of the information being revealed second-handed. Lockwood is an outsider who serves as the impetus for Nelly first to tell the story of Heathcliff and Catherine, and then to relate the story of their respective children.

In addition to Lockwood and Heathcliff, two servants are introduced in Chapter 1. The first is Joseph, an old man with a nasty disposition who has a sense of religious fanaticism; the other is only referred to as a "lusty dame" and is later identified as Zillah.

Literary Device

These characters are presented realistically, and other signs of realism are the depictions of the dogs and the details of the farmhouse furnishings. Brontë provides these kinds of details throughout the novel because having a sense of realism and authenticity is an important aspect of *Wuthering Heights*. Another important aspect is ownership of property, and even though the name "Hareton Earnshaw" is not explained, the family name plays an important part of *Wuthering Heights*. Because the opening chapter raises more questions than it answers, it serves as a hook to capture the attention of readers and encourage them to continue reading.

Glossary

(Here and in the following sections, difficult words and phrases are explained.)

misanthropist a person who hates or distrusts other people.

perseverance continued effort in spite of discouragement.

Go to the deuce go to the devil.

causeway a raised way over wet ground.

flags paving stones.

soliloquize to talk aloud to oneself.

ejaculation words spoken suddenly with emotion.

advent arrival.

wuthering exposed to the open air; here, used to describe the architecture of the farmhouse that endures assaults of nature (wind, snow, and rain).

grotesque artwork that distorts the usual human or animal form.

griffins animals with the head and wings of an eagle and the hind legs and tail of a lion.

countenance outward appearance.

gaiters leg coverings that reach to the mid-calf.

gypsy a member of a traditionally nomadic, or wandering, ethnic group.

vis-à-vis face to face.

physiognomy facial features.

phlegm indifference.

signet a mark left by a ring whose upper surface contains a signet, or seal, once used as a signature for marking documents.

Chapter 2

Summary

Lockwood returns to Wuthering Heights, and as he arrives, snow begins to fall. He knocks in vain, for, as Joseph explains, no one is willing or able to let him in. Eventually, a young man appears and beckons Lockwood to follow him. Once inside, Lockwood sees who he assumes is Heathcliff's wife and attempts to engage her in conversation. He does not succeed. Lockwood waits for Heathcliff's return, all the while making inaccurate assumptions and suppositions. The snowfall develops into a snowstorm, and Lockwood asks for assistance finding his way back to the Grange. Unable to get any help, he grabs a lantern that he says he will return in the morning. Joseph thinks he is stealing the lantern and commands the dogs to attack him. Lockwood ends up suffering a terrible nosebleed and is forced to spend the night at Wuthering Heights.

Commentary

Chapter 2 primary serves as an introduction to characters—Zillah, known formerly as only the "lusty dame" is now identified; Nelly Dean is mentioned but not named; Hareton Earnshaw (whose name matches the inscription over the door) is named but his presence is not explained; and the "missis" is introduced as Heathcliff's widowed daughter-in-law, though her first name is not mentioned either. In what is almost an aside, Joseph mentions the mother of Mrs. Heathcliff, claiming she went straight to the devil. Providing mostly exposition, the information is neither straightforward nor entirely explained, again creating a bit of mystery. Clearly these characters, who do not get along, let alone like one another, are somehow tied together.

Introducing these characters to the reader is Lockwood, who again serves as narrator of these events, although Nelly, the unnamed housekeeper, serves as the primary narrator for the majority of the novel. Immediately, Lockwood's reliability is again called into question. First of all, his decision to return to Wuthering Heights is itself questionable—he is not invited, the weather is poor, and he is not sure of the way. Yet, after he arrives, he is annoyed that the inhabitants are being inhospitable. He has unrealistic expectations, which he presumes will be met. When Hareton leads him inside, Lockwood waits for the "missis" to ask him to be seated, which of course she does not do. Hareton orders him to be seated, and in an attempt to make polite conversation, Lockwood misidentifies a heap of rabbit pelts as pets and misidentifies the woman as Heathcliff's wife. After being corrected by Heathcliff, Lockwood then mistakes Hareton as Heathcliff's son. Lockwood's inability to read people and situations make his narration suspect.

Character Insight

In addition to the development of Lockwood's character, important bits of information about other characters are revealed. Joseph, although fanatically religious, is also superstitious. Hareton is fiercely proud about his heritage. Mrs. Heathcliff is a paradoxical beauty who does not like being at Wuthering Heights but is not permitted to leave. And Heathcliff has lost both a wife and a son. At this point in time, these characters are intriguing but not sympathetic.

Glossary

N.B. [Latin *nota bene*] mark well; used to call attention to an item.

assiduity careful attention.

moors open rolling land that cannot be used for farming due to poor drainage.

sagacity keen or wise perception.

austere somber.

taciturn silent.

amiable good natured and pleasant.

diabolical very wicked or cruel.

box his ears slap him on the head.

Black Art witchcraft.

guffaw loud laughter.

copestone here, a finishing touch.

miscreants those having vicious behavior.

King Lear the title character in Shakespeare's tragedy *King Lear*; here, mentioned by Lockwood to show his education, distancing himself from the lower class.

copious very plentiful.

benevolent showing goodwill.

moroseness sullen mood.

Chapter 3

Summary

Zillah leads Lockwood to a chamber in which Heathcliff allows no one to stay. Lockwood discovers a bed hidden behind panels and decides to spend the night there, safe from Heathcliff. By candlelight Lockwood spots three names—*Catherine Earnshaw, Catherine Heathcliff,* and *Catherine Linton*—and some books. Unable to fall asleep, he glances through the mildewed books.

In one of the books, Lockwood finds a caricature of Joseph and many diary-type entries. The entries reveal that Catherine is friendly with Heathcliff and that her brother Hindley treats Heathcliff poorly. After reading several entries, Lockwood falls asleep and has two nightmares. He thinks a fir branch tapping on the windows awakened him from his first dream, and during the second he attempts to break off the branch.

In order to reach the branch, Lockwood pushes his hand through the window, but instead of grabbing a branch, he touches an ice-cold hand. As he struggles to free his hand from the cold grasp, a voice cries out "Let me in—let me in!" The voice identified itself as Catherine Linton. Unable to free himself from the ghost, he forces the wrist on the broken glass and tricks the ghost into letting go. As soon as he is free, Lockwood piles books against the hole. When they begin to topple, he screams.

Lockwood's crying out draws Heathcliff into the chambers. Lockwood declares the room haunted and as he leaves the room, he notices that Heathcliff is distraught by the mention of the name "Catherine" and is imploring the spirit to return. Lockwood finishes the night in the back-kitchen. As soon as it is dawn, he returns to the Grange. Heathcliff shows him the way home, and Lockwood arrives soaked and chilled.

Commentary

The name *Catherine* is mentioned for the first time. This name refers to the older Catherine (referred to as Catherine in this Note. Her daughter is also named Catherine and is referred to as Cathy in this Note). The three last names associated with it, in chronological order, mention the primary associations in Catherine Earnshaw's life. Maintaining symmetry in the text, when read in reverse order, they chronicle the life of Cathy.

Character Insight

In the diary entry about Hindley's treatment of Heathcliff, readers gain the first bit of insight into the enigmatic main character. Perhaps he is the product of his environment, rebelling against his tormentors. From Catherine's perspective, Hindley is far worse a person than Heathcliff could ever be. Throughout the novel, the primary characters, particularly Heathcliff and Catherine, tend to demonstrate two sides, and these revelations make it extremely difficult for readers to maintain a constant vision of them. In the first two chapters, Heathcliff seems to care about no one, yet, at the end of Chapter 3, he is clearly tormented about the loss of Catherine. Clearly, the man who is initially presented as cold and heartless has the ability to also be quite passionate.

An important question is determining the source of Heathcliff's passion—is it Catherine or the act of revenge? Brontë introduces the supernatural in this chapter, and readers need to determine if the ghost of Catherine has truly been walking the world 18 years, waiting for Heathcliff, or if she is an incredibly vivid product of Lockwood's imagination.

Lockwood's interaction with the ghost/dream is also quite revealing. Although many characters are said to be cruel to one another throughout *Wuthering Heights*, what he does, pulling the wrist on broken glass and "rub[bing] it to and fro till the blood ran down and soaked the bedclothes," is as cruel an action to another as any other character in the text. Lockwood's interaction with Catherine's spirit moves him from being an outside observer to an active participant in the plot.

Glossary

spectres   ghosts.

dilapidation   decay.

garret unfinished part of a house just under the roof.

palaver idle talk between two people.

pinafores sleeveless dresses or garments worn over dresses.

asseverated spoken earnestly.

lachrymose mournful.

vagabond an irresponsible wanderer.

cudgel a short club.

excommunicated excluded from church membership.

casement a window with side hinges that open outward.

changeling a child switched with another in infancy.

stagnate to be motionless.

impudence boldness.

sotto voce under one's breath, so as not to be overheard

egress an exit.

decorum polite behavior.

adieux good-byes.

Chapter 4

Summary

Recuperating from his wanderings, Lockwood asks Nelly about Heathcliff and his daughter-in-law. Nelly informs him that the widow's maiden name was Catherine Linton, the daughter of Nelly's late master, and that Hareton Earnshaw is the nephew of her late master's wife. Cathy is the last of the Lintons, and Hareton is the last of the Earnshaws. Nelly also reveals that Heathcliff had married Mr. Linton's sister.

This bit of information piques Lockwood's curiosity, so he encourages Nelly to tell him the history of the people and places he has encountered. Her story begins with her life at Wuthering Heights; she grew up with Catherine and Hindley Earnshaw. Mr. Earnshaw brought an orphan home from Liverpool, named him Heathcliff (after a son who died in childbirth), and grew to love the boy more than his own son.

Catherine and Hindley both initially disliked Heathcliff, but Catherine soon grew to love him. Hindley resented Heathcliff, especially for displacing him from his father. After Mrs. Earnshaw died, within two years of Heathcliff's arrival, Hindley was separated from everyone in his family.

Commentary

Lockwood's involvement with Catherine's spirit, as well as his interest in the Heathcliff, prompts him to ask Nelly Dean about the history of Wuthering Heights. At this point, Nelly assumes the role of primary narrator of the novel. During her narration, however, she often quotes other characters, so some of her information is not first-hand but rather second- and third-hand knowledge.

Her explanation about Heathcliff's introduction into the Earnshaw household provides sympathy for both Heathcliff and Hindley. From Hindley's perspective, Heathcliff has usurped the love of both his father and his sister. Heathcliff is an orphan who is ready to accept the members of a family that is not fully ready to accept him.

Theme

The childhood of both Catherine and Heathcliff provides the development of their characters and foreshadows their futures. When crossed, Catherine, the warm and loving daughter, can be defiant, headstrong, and cruel. Heathcliff can be brooding, sullen, and capable of vindictiveness. Their relationship begins to explore one of the primary themes of *Wuthering Heights*, namely that love can be capricious and its consequences, devastating.

Glossary

weather-cock here, a person who changes easily.

strike my colours here, surrender or give in.

indigenae native to a particular area.

near frugal.

churl rude, ill-bred person.

hob shelf in the side of a fireplace where an item can be kept warm.

flighted frightened.

bairns children.

usurper a person who wrongfully takes a possession or position.

insolent disrespectful.

cuffed slapped.

interloper an intruder.

qualm faintness or nausea.

vindictive seeking revenge.

Chapter 5

Summary

As Mr. Earnshaw's health begins to fail, he becomes less tolerant of complaints about Heathcliff, and as a result, sends Hindley away to school. As Mr. Earnshaw moves closer to death, Joseph begins to have a greater influence over his master, particularly in regard to religion.

Catherine continues to tease her father about her exploits with Heathcliff, never really conscious of how sick her father really is. When Mr. Earnshaw dies, Catherine and Heathcliff console one another with talk of heaven.

Commentary

The bond between Catherine and Heathcliff grows stronger as Mr. Earnshaw grows weaker. The extent of their love is shown as they console each other with talk of heaven the night Mr. Earnshaw dies. This is a particularly interesting scene because, although religious terms like *heaven* and *angel* are used to describe Catherine (and other religious terms, like *devil* and *Satan* are used to describe Heathcliff), neither character is shown to be particularly religious in a conventional understanding. It is as if the love Catherine and Heathcliff share is truly beyond organized religion and is indeed spiritual. Mr. Earnshaw's death, however, is the one time that Catherine and Heathcliff do not turn exclusively to one another. At this time, religious beliefs bring them comfort; at all other times, Catherine and Heathcliff serve as each other's source of love.

Glossary

curate [Archaic] a clergyman.

reprobate rejected as worthless.

frame go.

summut something.

Chapter 6

Summary

Hindley returns for his father's funeral and brings a wife, Frances, along with him. Taking control of the farmhouse, Hindley immediately makes changes, moving Joseph and Nelly to the back-kitchen and prohibiting Heathcliff from receiving an education. Hindley also makes Heathcliff work in the fields. Hindley does not pay much attention to either Heathcliff or Catherine, and so they live "as savages," skipping church and playing on the moors.

One day both Catherine and Heathcliff disappear. When they can not be found, Hindley orders the doors bolted. Nelly waits up for them, but finds out that Heathcliff returned home alone. He explains to Nelly that he and Catherine ended up near Thrushcross Grange and stole closer to peer into the windows and make fun of Edgar and Isabella, the Linton children. As Catherine and Heathcliff laugh at the Lintons, they are heard and run away. Skulker, the Linton's dog, chases after them, biting Catherine on the ankle.

Because of her injury, Catherine is unable to get away. A servant carries her into the Grange. Mr. and Mrs. Linton are shocked at the appearance and behavior of both Catherine and Heathcliff and are unwilling to allow Heathcliff to spend the night, even as they tend to Catherine's injury. Concerned for Catherine's safety, Heathcliff spies on them. He sees that they treat her like a queen. After a visit from Mr. Linton, who scolded Hindley about the manner in which he raised his sister, Hindley threatens Heathcliff with banishment the next time he so much as talks to Catherine.

Commentary

Literary Device

Being able to roam free across the moors best illustrates the wildness of Catherine and Heathcliff's natures. This rough freedom of Wuthering Heights contrasts with the dignified calmness of Thrushcross Grange. Similarly, the Linton children (safe, spoiled, and cowardly) serve as a contrast to Catherine and Heathcliff (self-willed, strong, and rebellious).

For the first time, a difference between Catherine and Heathcliff is revealed: She is drawn to the civility and luxury present there whereas he is repulsed by it. Ironically, Heathcliff is once again an outsider, meeting with rejection. Heathcliff will never be a welcome presence at Thrushcross Grange, but Catherine will always be treated as royalty.

Within Nelly's narration, the events that transpired at Thrushcross Grange are told from Heathcliff's point of view. He immediately dislikes the Lintons and what they represent, plus they now have what he cherishes most, namely Catherine. Therefore, the narrative once again becomes slightly suspect. Perhaps things occurred exactly as Heathcliff relates them or perhaps he paints a slightly skewed picture.

This chapter marks the first significant change in Catherine's character. She experiences a whole new world at Thrushcross Grange, a world that will not and cannot contain Heathcliff. Gradually the change in Catherine will lead to a change in the relationship between Catherine and Heathcliff, whether she wants it to or not.

Glossary

delf-case a cabinet for tableware named for popular glazed earthenware, usually blue and white, originating in the city of Delft.

peevish hard to please.

flogging a beating with a strap, stick, or whip, especially as punishment.

catechised taught, especially in the principles of religion, by the method of questions and answers.

slaver saliva drooling from the mouth.

beard to face or oppose courageously or brazenly.

strong-hold a place having strong defenses; here, Mr. Linton is referring to his home, Thrushcross Grange.

negus a hot beverage made from wine, hot water, and lemon juice, sweetened and spiced.

Chapter 7

Summary

Catherine remains at Thrushcross Grange for five weeks. During her stay, Mrs. Linton works with her, transforming the wild girl into a young lady. When Catherine returns to Wuthering Heights, she is barely recognizable. Hindley, treating Heathcliff as a servant, allows Catherine's playmate to step forward to greet her when she arrives. Catherine kisses Heathcliff, but while doing so, she comments upon his dirty appearance and compares him unfavorably to Edgar. Heathcliff is hurt by the changes in his friend's appearance and attitude.

Hindley invites the Lintons to dinner the following day, and they agree to visit, on the condition that the Linton children will not have to encounter Heathcliff. Hindley agrees to this condition, although Nelly convinces Heathcliff to make himself presentable. As the Lintons arrive, Hindley banishes Heathcliff to the kitchen. Edgar makes what Heathcliff considers an insulting comment about his appearance, and he throws hot applesauce in Edgar's face. Hindley has Heathcliff locked in the attic until dinner is over.

Catherine blames Edgar for getting Heathcliff in trouble, and after dinner, while the others are listening to music and dancing, she sneaks away to visit Heathcliff. Nelly ends up permitting Heathcliff to go into the kitchen for a bite to eat. While eating, Heathcliff tells Nelly that he is plotting revenge against Hindley.

Commentary

When Catherine returns to Wuthering Heights, the outward changes are readily apparent. Her demeanor toward Heathcliff is both understandable and expected; now, for the first time, she recognizes the differences in social standing. It is important to remember that differences in social class were constantly recognized and that the Lintons had more social standing than the Earnshaws.

Nelly presents Heathcliff in a most-sympathetic light, taking his side and encouraging him to clean himself up. When things do not turn out as planned, the resulting situation sets up the conflicts between Heathcliff and Hindley and between Heathcliff and Edgar that will permeate the rest of *Wuthering Heights*. For the first time, Heathcliff mentions his desire for revenge.

Glossary

mire deep mud.

discomfiture uneasiness.

dusky somewhat dark in color.

morrow the next day.

cant lass bold girl.

impertinence lack of proper respect or manners.

tureen a large, deep serving dish with a lid.

prognosticate to foretell or predict.

Chapter 8

Summary

During the following summer, Frances gives birth to Hareton, but Frances dies a week later because she had been suffering from consumption. Nelly is expected to take complete control of the newborn. Hindley is distraught over the death of his wife and becomes tyrannical, forcing all the servants but Nelly and Joseph away. He also begins to treat Heathcliff more cruelly, and Heathcliff delights in Hindley's downfall.

Catherine begins "to adopt a double character," behaving one way with Heathcliff and another with the Lintons. Heathcliff begins keeping track of how much time she is spending with Edgar and the Lintons, and he is angry that Catherine belittles him when he confronts her with this. Edgar arrives at the end of the argument.

Nelly keeps herself in the room with Catherine during Edgar's visit, and this annoys Catherine greatly. Unable to convince Nelly to leave, Catherine ends up pinching Nelly and then lies about it. Edgar tries to intervene, and Catherine boxes his ears. This is the first time he has seen the wild side of Catherine and he tells her that he must leave; however, on the way out, he sees Catherine through the window and returns. Later, Nelly interrupts the sweethearts to inform them that Mr. Earnshaw has returned home, drunk again.

Commentary

After his wife dies, Hindley starts a disintegration from which he never recovers. Avoiding his son and becoming a tyrannical drunkard, Hindley's demise serves as an eerie precursor to Heathcliff's own downfall. Heathcliff takes pleasure witnessing Hindley's self-destruction.

Character Insight

In addition to showing Heathcliff's delight in the downfall of others, this chapter, perhaps more than any other, reveals Nelly's genuine dislike of Catherine. She admits "I own I did not like her after her infancy was past" and claims she is "as bad as marred [spoiled] child." This admission immediately draws suspicion on her reliability. Clearly, at this point in time, she favors Heathcliff to Catherine, although this does not always remain constant.

Theme

A connection between love and cruelty surfaces in this chapter and is repeated constantly and consistently throughout *Wuthering Heights*. Those characters—especially Heathcliff—who exhibit the strongest love (that is, those who are most passionate) also tend to be the cruelest. Brontë explores this interconnection through the various types of relationships that she creates in *Wuthering Heights*.

Glossary

consumption a wasting away of the body, most likely tuberculosis.

rush of a lass a girl who is slender and delicate, like a rush.

infernal hellish; inhuman.

coquette a girl or woman who merely from vanity tries to get men's attention and admiration.

almanack [Archaic spelling] an almanac, a yearly calendar.

equanimity evenness of mind or temper.

assiduously with constant and careful attention.

consternation great fear or shock that makes one feel helpless or bewildered.

marred spoiled.

askance with a sideways glance.

Chapter 9

Summary

In a drunken rage, Hindley accidentally drops Hareton over the banister, but luckily, Heathcliff is present and catches the baby. Later, in the kitchen, Catherine speaks to Nelly. Thinking they are alone, Catherine tells Nelly that Edgar asked her to marry him and that she accepted. Catherine explains that she cannot marry Heathcliff because Hindley has degraded him so much; however, she expresses her love for Heathcliff. She prefaces her remarks with "It would degrade me to marry Heathcliff," and these are the words he overhears. Catherine continues, that Heathcliff will never know how much she loves him and that "he's more myself than I am."

Heathcliff leaves Wuthering Heights that night and disappears for three years. Catherine spends the entire night outdoors in the rain. She comes down with a bad chill, catches a fever, and almost dies. The Lintons allow her to recuperate at the Grange, but both Mr. and Mrs. Linton take the fever and die.

Three years after his parents' deaths, Edgar marries Catherine. They convince Nelly to leave Hareton and Wuthering Heights and move to Thrushcross Grange. When Nelly tries to refuse to go, both Edgar and Hindley force her to move.

Commentary

Catherine's dual nature reveals itself most fully in this chapter. In one breath she is able to declare her love for Heathcliff while simultaneously stating she cannot marry him. She agrees to marry Edgar yet naively thinks this marriage will not affect her relationship with Heathcliff. Catherine, like most of Victorian society, views marriage as a social contract and not the ultimate commitment between lovers. In her eyes, she and Heathcliff are one; therefore, her marriage to Edgar could not possibly affect the spiritual connection she has with Heathcliff.

Character Insight

In addition to their spiritual connection, a symbolic connection between Catherine and Heathcliff also exists. When Catherine arrives at Thrushcross Grange, she is as much an outsider there as Heathcliff was when he arrived at Wuthering Heights. Upon their arrivals, both reek havoc and turmoil on the inhabitants. Although Catherine chooses to marry and live with Edgar, she is out of her element.

Glossary

wisht hush.

shilling a former monetary unit of the United Kingdom, equal to 1/20 of a pound.

perdition [Archaic] complete and irreparable loss; ruin.

blasphemer one who speaks irreverently or profanely of or to God.

bairnies grat children wept.

mools earth of a grave.

Milo a famous Greek athlete who, caught by the tree he was trying to split, was eaten up by wild beasts; here, Catherine suggests that anyone who attempts to split Heathcliff and herself will end up destroyed.

settle a long wooden bench with a back, armrests, and sometimes a chest beneath the seat.

supplication a humble request, prayer, or petition.

vociferate to utter or shout loudly or vehemently.

Chapter 10

Summary

Heathcliff reappears suddenly one September afternoon, approximately six months after Catherine and Edgar marry. Nelly does not tell Catherine who the visitor is, but she does tell Edgar. Edgar suggests that Catherine visit in the kitchen, but she insists on entertaining in the parlor. Catherine's excitement over Heathcliff's return was not the reception he expected, but he is pleased to receive it. Their words and actions reveal that Catherine and Heathcliff love each other. Heathcliff surprises everyone by stating that he is staying at Wuthering Heights.

Catherine and Isabella often visit the Heights, and Heathcliff visits the Grange. During these visits, Isabella becomes infatuated with Heathcliff. He is not interested in the young lady, but he is interested in the fact that she is her brother's heir. Nelly is concerned about Heathcliff's return, vowing to watch for any signs of impropriety.

Commentary

Now the jealousy between Edgar and Heathcliff is out in the open. Catherine is clearly bored with Edgar and her life at the Grange, and her reaction to Heathcliff's arrival bothers Edgar as much as it pleases Heathcliff. And Catherine enjoys the attention. As Edgar's wife, she is able to be the socialite; as Heathcliff's love, she is able to be true to her innermost desires and passions.

Literary Device

Many questions exist: How did Heathcliff transform himself? Is the transformation only external? What is the source of his money? Why is he staying at Wuthering Heights, with Hindley, whom he hates? Where Heathcliff was and what he was doing is never answered, but readers soon find out that his transformation is indeed only skin-deep and he has not forgotten his revenge against Hindley. Heathcliff also reveals his greed, which foreshadows the extent he will go to take revenge on Edgar as well.

Glossary

dilatory inclined to delay; slow or late in doing things.

sizer's place a student receiving a scholarship allowance at Trinity College, Dublin, or at Cambridge University.

imperious overbearing, arrogant, or domineering.

averred declared to be true; stated positively.

fastidiousness the state of being refined in a too dainty or oversensitive way, so as to be easily disgusted.

degradation the state of being lower in rank, status, or condition.

trifles things of little value or importance.

abjured gave up.

superfluous not needed; unnecessary.

furze a prickly evergreen shrub.

mawkish nauseating.

Chapter 11

Summary

Nelly ventures back to Wuthering Heights to talk with Hindley; instead she encounters Hareton, who has no memory of her. Hareton greets her with a barrage of stones and curses—actions he learned from Heathcliff. When Heathcliff appears, Nelly runs away.

The next day at the Grange, Nelly witnesses an embrace between Heathcliff and Isabella. When Catherine confronts Heathcliff about this, he tells her "I'm not *your* husband: *you* needn't be jealous of me." This leads Heathcliff to reveal that he knows Catherine has wronged him and that he will be revenged.

Edgar confronts both Catherine and Heathcliff. Catherine ends ups locking the door and taunting her husband into a fair fight between Heathcliff and himself. Edgar ends up hitting Heathcliff in the throat and rushes off to get assistance. Realizing he cannot fight three men with weapons, Heathcliff leaves.

Edgar then demands that Catherine choose between Heathcliff and himself. Catherine doesn't answer. Instead, she locks herself in her room, refusing to eat for two days. Unable to get through to Catherine, Edgar informs Isabella that if she were to pursue a relationship with Heathcliff, that action would signify the end of their relationship.

Commentary

Heathcliff is now acting as both father and teacher to Hareton. This assumption of the paternal role mirrors the way Hindley assumed Mr. Earnshaw's role as father to Heathcliff, and then immediately lessened Heathcliff's status at Wuthering Heights. Now, Heathcliff has taken both Hindley's father and son away from him. Hindley ended Heathcliff's formal education at Wuthering Heights; Heathcliff does the same to Hareton. This is the first part of Heathcliff's master plan for revenge.

After working his way back into Wuthering Heights, Heathcliff aims for Thrushcross Grange, directing the second part of his revenge towards Edgar by encouraging Isabella's infatuation. Heathcliff has no passion, love, or desire for Isabella; he only wants to use her. And he does. Having been so ceremoniously removed from Thrushcross Grange as a child, Heathcliff desires to acquire it, and Isabella supplies the means for him to do this.

Literary Device

Catherine's hysterics followed by her refusal to eat illustrate both her weakening mental and physical self. When she locks Edgar and Heathcliff together and throws the key into the fire, this is the height of romanticism for her. Symbolically, that key represents the key to her heart. She throws it away, and in doing so, actually pushes both men away. Edgar cannot understand her love for someone so crass and wild as Heathcliff; Heathcliff cannot fathom her attraction to the sniveling and weak Edgar. Curiously, Edgar is the one who acts out of character by striking Heathcliff. This action demonstrates the lengths that Edgar will go for the woman he loves.

Glossary

approbation official approval, sanction, or commendation.

acquiesced agreed or consented quietly without protest, but without enthusiasm.

vanquished defeated.

recriminate to answer an accuser by accusing that person in return; reply with a countercharge.

stolidity the state of showing little or no emotion.

compunction a sharp feeling of uneasiness brought on by a sense of guilt.

Chapter 12

Summary

After three days of starving herself, Catherine agrees to eat. She is distraught that she is dying and Edgar has not come to her, begging forgiveness. In a state of delirium, Catherine talks about her childhood with Heathcliff and speaks of her impending death. When Nelly refuses to open the window, Catherine staggers to it, throws it open, and claims to see Wuthering Heights.

In her next breath, she speaks of being buried but not at rest until she is with Heathcliff. Edgar finds Catherine in such a weakened condition and admonishes Nelly for not calling him sooner. She in turn goes to seek medical attention. During this same night, Isabella runs away with Heathcliff. The doctor arrives and predicts that Catherine will not survive this illness. Edgar, when hearing about his sister's actions, says she is now a sister in name only.

Commentary

Again in this chapter, Nelly's reliability is called into question. Early in the chapter she is convinced that "the Grange had but one sensible soul in its walls, and that lodged in my body." This attitude not only demonstrates a sense of superiority but also provides a means of validating all of her questionable actions, thus limiting her own responsibility. At the end of the chapter she does not want to be "blamed for another's wicked waywardness." Nelly sees herself as Catherine's superior and determines that Catherine has no one but herself to blame for the state she is in.

Character Insight

As Catherine's condition deteriorates, essential aspects of her character are revealed. First and foremost, Catherine admits to Nelly "I'm afraid of being alone." Catherine is used to having someone—whether it was her father, Nelly, Heathcliff, or Edgar—tending to her every need and whim. She does not recognize that her actions and decisions are precisely why she is alone.

She makes other important revelations, such as her longing to be outside, playing like a child on the moors and claiming, "I won't rest till you [Heathcliff] are with me." Close to death, Catherine longs for the time in her life when she was most happy—her childhood. Her comments about not resting foreshadow the restlessness Heathcliff experiences after her death, illustrating yet again the connection they have with one another.

Catherine is most cruel when she is most honest, telling her husband, "I don't want you, Edgar; I'm past wanting you." She expected Edgar to tend to her in her weakened state, oblivious to the torment and anguish to which she has subjected him. Edgar did not meet her timetable and therefore, is no longer needed. In a way, Catherine enjoys playing the martyr, feeling she will suffer for her love.

Glossary

pertinaciously stubbornly.

gruel thin, easily digested porridge made by cooking meal in water or milk.

elf-bolts flint arrowheads.

paroxysm a sudden outburst.

tumult confusion.

Chapter 13

Summary

Edgar nurses Catherine for the next two months. During this time, it is revealed that Catherine is pregnant. Edgar longs for a male heir, to prevent Heathcliff and Isabella from inheriting the Grange.

Six weeks after she runs away, Isabella sends a letter to Edgar, announcing her marriage and begging forgiveness. He does not reply. After that, a distraught Isabella sends a letter to Nelly, questioning the humanity of Heathcliff. She tells Nelly that they are living at Wuthering Heights and begs for a visit. The letter goes on to tell of her experiences at Wuthering Heights. Isabella encounters Hareton, Joseph, and Hindley: All are rude and uncaring. She realizes her mistake but also knows that it is too late. She cannot even find a place to sleep that is her own. When Heathcliff returns, he tells her that Catherine is sick, that he blames Edgar, and that he plans on making her suffer in place of Edgar.

Commentary

Nearing death, Catherine knows the next time she goes to the moors will be her last. She does not allow Edgar to comfort either her or himself with a false sense of hope or security. Edgar nurses Catherine tenderly and attentively as best he can, but is he doing this out of love for his wife or the child she is bearing? Without an heir, Isabella would inherit Thrushcross Grange in the event of Edgar's death. Because Isabella is married to Heathcliff, that means Edgar's rival would essentially inherit Edgar's property. Edgar does not want this to happen.

While Edgar is nursing Catherine, readers get a view of Heathcliff from Isabella's perspective. Her letter to Nelly narrates the events that have transpired from the time she eloped. Isabella questions if Heathcliff is really a man and suggests that he may be incarnate evil. She realizes marrying him was a mistake but also realizes she cannot atone for her error. Isabella reveals that Heathcliff blames Edgar for Catherine's suffering, and he will take this out on Isabella, too. Heathcliff may or may not be the devil, but he is making Isabella's life a living hell.

Glossary

frame off be gone.

soliloquy an act or instance of talking aloud to oneself.

thible a smooth stick for stirring broth or porridge.

vouchsafed was gracious enough, or condescended, to give or grant.

adjuration an earnest entreaty or request.

abhorrence loathing, detestation.

Chapter 14

Summary

Edgar refuses to forgive Isabella and sends nothing with Nelly when Nelly visits Wuthering Heights. Heathcliff is eager to hear news of Catherine's situation and demands that Nelly arrange a meeting between the two. Nelly refuses, but her refusal prompts Heathcliff to force Nelly to stay at Wuthering Heights, claiming he will go alone. Nelly fears what might happen if that were to occur and begrudgingly agrees to his request to carry a letter to Catherine.

Commentary

Of particular importance in this chapter is Heathcliff's declaration and explanation of his love for Catherine. Heathcliff tells Nelly, "For every thought she [Catherine] spends on Linton, she spends a thousand on me . . . If he [Edgar] loved with all the powers of his puny being, he couldn't love as much in eighty years as I could in a day." The passion and commitment Heathcliff reveals frightens Nelly and is partially the reason he is able to persuade her to carry a letter to Catherine.

As Heathcliff discusses his relationship to both Catherine and Isabella, he appears to be true to himself: He recognizes that he is brutal and cruel. He is, however, also intelligent and manipulative, which is how he is able to con Nelly into agreeing to do his bidding.

Glossary

epistle a letter, especially a long, formal instructive letter.

sideboard dining-room furniture for holding linen, silver, and china.

perspicacity keen judgement or understanding.

brach [Archaic] a female hound.

appellation the act of calling by a name.

dree to endure or suffer; here, it is used to characterize sadness.

Chapter 15

Summary

Four days later, Nelly delivers the letter, while the rest of the household is at church. Catherine is close to death and cannot even hold it. Nelly tells her it is from Heathcliff, but before Nelly can call him to the room (he is lurking around the Grange), Heathcliff bursts into the room.

When Catherine sees him, she claims that both Edgar and he have broken her heart. She laments dying while he is still alive and longs for them never to be parted. An emotional reunion, of sorts, takes place, and they embrace. After the embrace Heathcliff speaks harshly to Catherine, saying, "You deserve this. You have killed yourself."

Distraught, Catherine sobs that "I forgive you. Forgive me!"

Holding her responsible for breaking both of their hearts, Heathcliff considers her the murderer of both of them and tells her, "I forgive what you have done to me. I love *my* murderer—but *yours!* How can I?"

Edgar returns from church services at this time, but as Heathcliff prepares to leave, Catherine begs him to stay. He consents. Nelly cries out; Edgar quickens his pace; Catherine collapses. As Edgar bursts into the room, Heathcliff puts Catherine's body into Edgar's arms, begging him to take care of her before he attacks Heathcliff. Nelly makes Heathcliff leave, promising to give him word about her condition in the morning.

Commentary

Ironically, at the start of the chapter, Lockwood claims Nelly to be "a very fair narrator," yet he has proven himself to be a bad judge of character, so his words should not be all that reassuring for the discerning reader. Reliability aside, Nelly continues the narrative.

Literary
Device

What Catherine says and does not say reveals telling and compelling information about her character. She tells Heathcliff, "You and Edgar have broken my heart," placing the blame at their feet. But while she is being open and honest with Heathcliff, not once does she say she regrets marrying Edgar. Her comments about not being at peace and about Heathcliff's happiness when she is buried foreshadows her ghost walking the world for eighteen years, haunting Heathcliff.

After rambling for a while, Catherine begs forgiveness, but Heathcliff cannot or will not give it. Perhaps this lack of forgiveness is what haunts him: The memory that he did not fully forgive her on her deathbed may be the worst of all the terrible things he has done in his life. Catherine herself alludes to this possibility when she says, "if you nurse anger, that will be worse to remember than my harsh words!" Perhaps only in her last moments of life does Catherine come to a true understanding of love.

At the end of the chapter, when Catherine collapses into Heathcliff's arms and Nelly thinks Catherine has died, Nelly remarks "Far better that she should be dead, than lingering a burden and a misery-maker to all about her." These cold and callous comments reveal the truth about Nelly and her feelings, just as Heathcliff giving Catherine's body to Edgar, placing Catherine's needs ahead of his own, reveal the truth about the depths of his love. For Nelly, Catherine's death will be a blessing, a lessening of a burden; for Heathcliff, Catherine's death is the beginning of his own personal hell.

Glossary

vindictiveness the state of being revengeful in spirit, and inclined to seek vengeance.

Chapter 16

Summary

At midnight that night, Catherine's daughter Cathy is born two months prematurely; two hours later, Catherine dies. In the morning, Nelly seeks Heathcliff to tell him the news, but he is already aware of the situation. He is angered that Catherine did not mention his name in her dying moments and is despondent over losing her. He simultaneously curses her spirit while lamenting his loss.

Edgar watches over Catherine's body by day; Heathcliff watches over it by night. Heathcliff replaces a lock of Edgar's hair from the trinket around Catherine's neck with some of his own. Nelly finds the strands of Edgar's hair and ends up intertwining both his and Heathcliff's with hers. To everyone's surprise, Catherine is buried in the churchyard, by a low wall, just feet from the moors.

Commentary

Edgar suffers two losses in this chapter—the death of his wife and the birth of a non-heir. Because Cathy is not a male, she legally is not Edgar's heir, and complicated laws end up leaving Thrushcross Grange to Isabella, and then to her son. This is not to suggest that Edgar does not love Cathy; he adores her, and she is his world. He just hates the fact that his rival may end up with his property.

With the shock of Catherine's death, Heathcliff implores her to haunt him: "I *cannot* live without my life! I *cannot* live without my soul!" He is clearly devastated by the death of his one true love, and although Heathcliff has done dastardly deeds throughout the text, most readers tend to sympathize with him and the loss he is feeling.

Edgar is devastated too, but by burying Catherine near her beloved moors, Edgar demonstrates both the depth of his love for his wife as well as insight into understanding her character. He wants Catherine to be happy and at peace, and this is one final gesture he can give to show his love.

Glossary

suffused overspread so as to fill with a glow.

goaded driven by a strong impulse.

interment burial.

Chapter 17

Summary

Quite unexpectedly, Isabella arrives at the Grange in a state of physical disarray. She knows better than to think Edgar will allow her to stay, so she is not seeking refuge, just assistance. She tells Nelly that Hindley stayed sober to attend his sister's funeral, but lost his courage and started drinking the morning of the service. When Heathcliff returns to Wuthering Heights from keeping vigil at Catherine's grave, Hindley locks him out of the house and tells Isabella that he is going to kill Heathcliff. Isabella tells Heathcliff of Hindley's intentions but does not allow him entrance to the house.

Heathcliff bursts into the house through a window and ends up beating Hindley. The next morning Isabella accuses Heathcliff of being responsible for everyone's misery and tells Hindley how Heathcliff beat him. Heathcliff and Hindley begin fighting again as Isabella makes her escape. After telling her story to Nelly, she leaves for London. She ends up giving birth to a son, Linton. Edgar and she begin corresponding, though he withdraws from society. Thirteen years later, Isabella dies.

Hindley dies six months after Catherine's death, and Nelly returns to Wuthering Heights to check on both funeral arrangements and Hareton. Nelly finds out that Hindley was deep in debt and that Heathcliff held the mortgage. Heathcliff refuses to allow Hareton to go with Nelly, threatening to take possession of Linton.

Commentary

In contrast to the previous chapter, all sympathy that readers gained for Heathcliff is lost when Heathcliff beats Hindley. During the beating, Hindley is the victim of his own past sins and Heathcliff's displaced anger and aggression about Catherine's death.

Soon after Catherine's death, Hindley dies too. The details are not exactly revealed, but Heathcliff claims Hindley "spent the night in drinking himself to death deliberately." Suicide is more probable than murder because Heathcliff had the chance to kill Hindley before but never did so.

Heathcliff has rough intentions with both Linton and Hareton. He refers to his own son as "it," not even affording Linton the level of respect of a person. And Heathcliff essentially steals Wuthering Heights from Hareton. Hareton is the rightful landowner, although the land is in debt. What Hareton should have inherited from his father is a mountain of debt with Heathcliff serving as the mortgagee. What happens, though, is Heathcliff assuming control of the property because he owns the mortgage.

This chapter marks the end of the first generation and the first half of *Wuthering Heights*. At this point in time, Heathcliff and Hareton are at Wuthering Heights, and Edgar and Cathy are at Thrushcross Grange. The second half of the novel in many ways mirrors the first, with Heathcliff longing for revenge, and willing to destroy anyone who is in his way.

Glossary

despot anyone in charge who acts like a tyrant.

sceptre a rod or staff, highly ornamented, held by rulers on ceremonial occasions as a symbol of sovereignty.

stanchion an upright bar, beam, or post used as a support.

odious arousing or deserving hatred or loathing.

ruffian a brutal, violent, lawless person; hoodlum.

preter-human beyond that which is human; especially, superhuman.

recapitulation a brief repetition, as in an outline; a summary.

malevolence spitefulness; ill will.

ardent warm or intense in feeling; passionate.

flaying whipping.

inveterate settled in a habit, practice, or prejudice; habitual.

carrion dead flesh.

Chapter 18

Summary

Young Cathy, sporting features of both parents, grows up at the Grange, unaware of Wuthering Heights and the people who live there. For 13 years Edgar never allows her to leave the grounds by herself. Being an inquisitive girl, when she hears of the Fairy cave at Penistone Craggs, she begs her father to take her there, but the road passes by Wuthering Heights, and he is not willing to travel there.

During the time of Cathy's fixation with the Fairy cave, Isabella writes to Edgar, informing him of her impending death. She asks him to come to her and take Linton to the Grange, in an attempt to keep him from Heathcliff. Edgar goes to her, leaving Nelly in charge of Cathy.

Nelly entertains Cathy by indulging in imaginative adventures about the grounds, but one morning, Cathy does not return. Seeking her out, Nelly discovers that Cathy's pony leaped the hedges this morning, heading in the general direction of Penistone Craggs.

Nelly ends up finding Cathy at Wuthering Heights. Cathy was riding toward the cave when Hareton's dogs and hers ended up getting intertwined. Hareton and Cathy spend the day together, enjoying themselves immensely—until Nelly arrives. Nelly insists on getting Cathy home immediately, but she is too interested in Hareton. Her interest vanishes, though, as soon as she finds out that Hareton is not the son of the master of Wuthering Heights. She immediately assumes he is a servant, and this enrages Hareton.

A servant reveals that Hareton is Cathy's cousin; Cathy, in turn, reveals that her father is off to London to fetch her cousin. Both bits of news upset Nelly. She and Cathy decide not to tell Edgar of Cathy's visit because neither wants Nelly to lose her position at the Grange.

Commentary

Nelly starts the second half of her narrative focusing on her own self-preservation. She uses guilt to get Cathy to agree to keep the visit to Wuthering Heights a secret rather than to admit to Edgar what had happened. Although Nelly was not entirely at fault for Cathy's excursion, she finds it easier to pretend the entire incident did not exist because it is easier to avoid the truth than deal with any recriminations.

When Cathy is visiting Wuthering Heights, readers first receive a glimpse of Hareton's pride; he is reminiscent of young Heathcliff. In fact, many things are reminiscent of the earlier generation: The day Hareton and Cathy spend together at Penistone Craggs parallels the fun-filled adventures Heathcliff and Catherine had on the moors, and Cathy's rejection of Hareton's lack of an education mirrors her mother's rejection of Heathcliff's societal standing.

Glossary

propensity a natural inclination or tendency.

perverse obstinately disobedient or difficult.

emissaries persons or agents, especially a secret agents, sent on a specific mission.

galloway one of a small but strong breed of horses peculiar to Galloway, Scotland.

wicket a small door or gate.

propitiate to win or regain the goodwill of.

offald ways used to characterize Catherine's and Heathcliff's behavior as disreputable.

comminations threats or denunciations.

near stingy.

Chapter 19

Summary

Linton arrives from London, a "pale, delicate, effeminate boy" who greatly resembles Edgar. He is too weak and sick to play with Cathy and has to lie on a couch instead of sitting with the family during tea. Cathy treats him as should would a new pet. Edgar confides in Nelly that he hopes having a playmate his own age will help, if Heathcliff allows Linton to live at the Grange. Edgar's fears are realized when Joseph arrives that evening, demanding to take Linton to Wuthering Heights. Refusing to awaken Linton, Edgar promises Joseph that Linton will be delivered to Heathcliff in the morning.

Commentary

Although Cathy is excited about the imminent arrival of her "real" cousin (she does not want to consider Hareton a relative of hers), she is extremely disappointed in Linton. Cathy and the readers' first impressions are both similar and accurate. Linton's condition will not improve, especially living at Wuthering Heights.

As the second-generation characters develop in the second half of *Wuthering Heights*, readers should note significant similarities and differences between parents and their children. Most noticeably, although Linton's physical condition is nothing like Heathcliff's, he clearly reflects his father's tyrannical personality. Cathy, in turn, seems to possess the wildness of her mother, but her personality is tempered a bit, reflecting the nature of her father. Hareton's features favor his Aunt Catherine, but due to Heathcliff's upbringing, his personality is that of a young Heathcliff.

Glossary

sanguine optimistic; hopeful.

cap and mantle hat and cloak.

Chapter 20

Summary

The next morning, Nelly takes Linton to Wuthering Heights. In order to get him to go to a father that he does not know, Nelly makes all sorts of assurances that she knows are not true. When they arrive, Heathcliff refers to his son as "property" and, speaking directly to Linton, refers to the boy's mother as a "wicked slut." Although Heathcliff readily admits he does not love his son, he relishes the opportunity to gain access of the Grange through him. Nelly leaves as Linton cries out, "Don't leave me! I'll not stay here!"

Commentary

Nelly lies quite easily to Linton and is probably somewhat relieved that she will not have to deal with him. Undoubtedly, raising Linton would be worse than raising Catherine was. As Heathcliff refers to his son as "property," readers may slightly sympathize with Linton's predicament. Heathcliff clearly has no tolerance for his weak offspring, and the fact that Linton's looks favor his Uncle Edgar make Heathcliff hate him even more. The only use Heathcliff has for the "whey-faced whining wretch" is implementing his revenge against Edgar.

Glossary

trepidation fearful uncertainty.

puling whimpering or whining.

whelp a youth or child; a term usually showing contempt.

victuals articles of food, especially when prepared for use.

mucky dirty.

Chapter 21

Summary

Three years later, with the memory of Linton erased from her mind, Cathy and Nelly are both bird hunting and exploring on the moors. Cathy moves more quickly than Nelly does, and before Nelly can stop them, Cathy is speaking with Heathcliff. While speaking with Heathcliff, Cathy notices Hareton and remarks that she has met him before. Heathcliff cannot respond to that, but he does mention that she has met his son before and encourages Cathy and Nelly to visit his house.

Nelly knows that this is not a good idea but is unable to convince Cathy not to go because Cathy is eager to determine who Heathcliff's son is. Heathcliff mentions to Nelly his desire to have the cousins fall in love and get married. When Cathy and Linton do meet, they do not recognize each other at first. Although Linton is now taller than Cathy is, he is still quite sickly. Unwilling to show Cathy around the farmhouse at first, Linton stays inside while Hareton leaves to show his cousin Wuthering Heights.

Heathcliff sends Linton after his cousins, and as he leaves, Nelly hears Cathy mock Hareton's inability to read.

The next day, Cathy reveals everything about her visit to her father. Edgar tries to explain to Cathy why he kept her from her cousins and her uncle, but she does not understand his reasoning. Edgar also commands his daughter not to have any contact with Linton. This upsets Cathy greatly, and she begins to have a secret, letter-writing relationship with Linton. Nelly discovers what Cathy has been doing and destroys Linton's letters to Cathy, but Nelly does not tell Edgar.

Commentary

Heathcliff reveals his plan to Nelly and the readers, along with his rationale that he is doing this, only as a safeguard against legal disputes. It is interesting that he still considers Nelly a confidant. Often, in the past, she took his side, and he clearly still thinks he can manipulate her.

He is correct in his assumptions, for as he convinces Cathy to seek out his son, Nelly's chief concern is that Edgar will find out of the visit, and she laments "and I shall have the blame."

Literary Device

After Heathcliff reveals his plan and Nelly counters that Cathy would be Edgar's heir, Heathcliff's response foreshadows the fact that Edgar's lawyer is now on Heathcliff's payroll, for Heathcliff knows that "there is no clause in the will to secure it so." The only way he could know what Edgar's will stated is by being privy to it. And there is no way that Edgar would have allowed Heathcliff to know the contents of his will; therefore, Edgar's lawyer must have shown Heathcliff, or at least shared the contents.

When Nelly and Cathy arrive at Wuthering Heights, Linton has grown but is still as disagreeable as ever. He joins Cathy in making fun of Hareton's lack of a formal education and whines about not being able to travel the four miles to Thrushcross Grange. Logically, he argues, he is too sick to travel; therefore, Cathy must visit him.

Once again, Nelly's priorities seem to be skewed. Instead of telling Edgar about Cathy's letter writing, she takes it upon herself to burn them all, only threatening to tell Edgar. Nelly keeps Cathy's secret the same way that Cathy kept Nelly's secret (in Chapter 18); thus acting as Cathy's friend. Nelly will not always keep Cathy's secrets, as readers soon find out.

Glossary

baca tobacco.

hillock a small hill.

nab an abrupt termination of a range of uplands.

chit an immature or childish girl.

salubrious promoting health or welfare; wholesome.

paltry practically worthless.

vapid uninteresting or lifeless.

bathos descent from the lofty to the commonplace; here, Heathcliff remarks on how he has lessened Hareton's place in society.

Chapter 22

Summary

During the winter, Cathy has little time to think of Linton because she is nursing her father, whom she thinks is dying. While walking one day, Cathy's hat blows over the garden wall. Nelly helps Cathy over the wall to fetch it, but Cathy cannot scale the other side by herself. While Nelly searches for a key to open the gate, Heathcliff appears. He chides Cathy for writing letters to Linton for a few months and then suddenly stopping. He claims that she is playing games with Linton's affection and that he is now dying of a broken heart. Heathcliff tells Cathy that he will be away for a week and encourages her to visit her cousin. Cathy feels extremely guilty about what Heathcliff has told her, so she and Nelly take off for Wuthering Heights the next morning.

Commentary

Again, Nelly is convinced to do something that she should probably not do—escorting Cathy to Wuthering Heights. Nonetheless, Cathy is determined to prove her loyalty to her sick cousin, and is eager to dote on him. Nelly's own devotion to Cathy illustrates the difference between Catherine and her daughter. Because of Catherine's selfishness and willfulness, Nelly had no trouble contradicting Catherine and making her life miserable, but with Cathy, Nelly's actions are different. Nelly is truly fond of Cathy and therefore has very little difficulty rationalizing a way to agree to Cathy's requests.

Glossary

sackless feeble.

Michaelmas the feast of the archangel Michael, September 29.

diurnal occurring each day; daily.

Slough of Despond deep despair or dejection; from the "Slough of Despond" in John Bunyan's *Pilgrim's Progress*.

Chapter 23

Summary

Nelly and Cathy travel in the rain all the way to Wuthering Heights. Heathcliff is indeed not home, and Linton is more pathetic than ever. He complains about the servants and whines to Cathy, first for not visiting, and then for writing instead of visiting. He also mentions the idea of marriage. Linton's talk of love vexes Cathy, and she pushes his chair, sending him into a coughing fit. He uses this to claim that she injured him and worsened his condition; he guilts her into thinking she can nurse him back to health. Because Nelly catches a cold due to spending the day traveling in wet weather, Cathy spends her days nursing both Nelly and her father, but, unbeknownst to Nelly and Edgar, she spends her nights riding across the moors to visit Linton.

Commentary

For many critics, Nelly's sickness is a contrived plot point that is entirely too convenient to be believable; however, most critics concede that sickness was possible if not plausible. Therefore, it does not detract greatly from the narrative and does aid the advancement of Heathcliff's plan for revenge.

Instrumental in Heathcliff's plan is for Cathy to marry Linton, and in order for that to happen, he needs her to care for him. When Cathy discusses her attraction to Linton, her words echo her mother: "he'll soon do as I direct him with some slight coaxing." Cathy, like her mother, enjoys the notion of having control over a man.

Glossary

elysium any place or condition of ideal bliss or complete happiness.

contrite repentant.

scuttle a kind of a bucket, usually with a wide lip, used for pouring.

Chapter 24

Summary

After Nelly recovers, she notices that Cathy is agitated in the evening. Cathy pretends to retire early, but when Nelly cannot find her anywhere in the house, she waits in Cathy's room for her to return. Cathy attempts a feeble lie at first but soon admits the truth.

On one of her visits, Hareton stops her and tells her that he can read the name above the door; however, Cathy asks if he knows the numbers, and when he concedes he does not, she again makes fun of him. This enrages Hareton, and during her visit with Linton, Hareton storms into the room and forces Linton upstairs. Later Hareton attempts to apologize to Cathy, but she refuses to listen to him.

Cathy visits three days later, but Linton blames her for the previous trouble, so she leaves. When she returns two days later, she tells Linton this is her last visit, but this news causes him trouble, and he apologizes for his behavior.

Nelly listens to Cathy's tale, and then immediately tells Edgar everything. He forbids Cathy to continue visiting Linton but says he will write and invite Linton to visit the Grange.

Commentary

In this chapter Cathy serves as the primary narrator, telling Nelly (who in turn tells Lockwood) about her evening visits to Wuthering Heights. Many readers question Cathy's devotion to Linton, for he does not seem particularly agreeable. Again, Cathy ridicules Hareton, but this time her words lead to an injury for Linton. Unbelievably, this is an incident that Linton holds Cathy accountable for. In doing so, he is remaining true to his self-centered, annoying character.

Nelly, however, abruptly changes her character. For the first time, she does the responsible, adult thing and tells Edgar almost everything about Cathy and Linton's developing relationship. What she does not tell him, however, is the extent of Linton's illness, and this ends up providing Edgar a false sense of security that his daughter might eventually marry and keep her family home.

Glossary

blind man's bluff a game in which a blindfolded player has to catch and identify another player.

niver never.

dunnut be 'feard don't be afraid.

allas summt always something.

Chapter 25

Summary

Breaking from her narrative, Nelly tells Lockwood that these events transpired a little over a year ago. Lockwood is so enraptured with the story that he begs her to continue.

Cathy obeys her father's wishes. Nelly tells Edgar that Linton is of frail health, and Edgar admits that he fears for Cathy's happiness. He even concedes that if marrying Linton would make Cathy happy, he would be in favor of it, even though it means Heathcliff would get what he wants.

Although Linton never visits the Grange, after much pleading, Edgar allows Cathy to visit with Linton on the moors.

Commentary

This short chapter is important for two significant reasons. First, it establishes the time frame, the previous winter, which is relatively close to Lockwood's arrival, and second, it establishes Edgar's mindset shortly before his death.

Because the current events just occurred the previous winter, the characters who Lockwood encounters at Wuthering Heights may still be closely affected by the events that have transpired. Recall that at Lockwood's visit to Wuthering Heights, Heathcliff had just recently lost his son and Cathy, her husband, and the way they reacted to the loss was indicative about their natures.

Edgar, now and up to the time of his death, remains misguided. He only wants Cathy's happiness, but happiness is something he was unable to provide for her mother, and it is something that he is unable to provide for their daughter.

Glossary

avaricious greedy for riches.

Chapter 26

Summary

At the time of the first scheduled meeting on the moors, Linton is not at the agreed-upon spot; rather, he is quite close to Wuthering Heights. Both Nelly and Cathy are concerned about Linton's health, but he insists that he is getting stronger. During their entire visit he is squeamish and scared and is constantly looking back towards his house. When it is time to leave, Cathy assures Linton that she promises to meet him again next Thursday. On the way home Cathy and Nelly discuss Linton's health and decide to wait until the next visit to determine the extent of his deterioration.

Commentary

Cathy has mixed emotions about meeting her cousin and senses that Heathcliff is the one pushing for them to meet. Readers, who already know of Heathcliff's plans, realize that Cathy has a reason to be cautious.

Literary Device

Linton is clearly dying, yet his father is still using him as a means of revenge. Nelly's inability to reveal anything to Edgar foreshadows the forthcoming abduction.

Glossary

pertinacious persistent.

bilberries any of several North American species of blueberries.

Chapter 27

Summary

During the week that follows, Edgar's health continues to deteriorate, so it is grudgingly that Cathy rides to meet Linton. During the visit, Heathcliff arrives and demands to know if Edgar is truly dying. Heathcliff is worried that Linton might die before Edgar does.

Heathcliff asks Cathy to walk her cousin back to Wuthering Heights. Although she meekly reminds Heathcliff that she is forbidden from visiting the farmhouse, Cathy disobeys her father's instructions. Linton's cries of anguish and Heathcliff's rage, which is directed toward Linton, however, convince both Cathy and Nelly to accompany them.

After they're inside, Heathcliff imprisons Cathy and Nelly; he will not release her until after she and Linton are married. Overnight, Heathcliff locks Cathy in a bedroom. In the morning he frees Cathy from the room, but Nelly is held prisoner for five days, only seeing Hareton, who serves as her jailer.

Commentary

Linton is extremely pathetic and obviously terrified of Heathcliff; however, the manner in which he speaks to Cathy after she is lured to Wuthering Heights mitigates any sympathy readers may be feeling for him.

After Cathy is locked inside, Linton reveals to her Heathcliff's plans, and a sense of inescapable doom exists. This kidnapping, the first time Heathcliff does something entirely outside the limits of the law, is an act of desperation on his behalf; Linton needs to marry Cathy before Edgar's death, and Edgar needs to die before Linton does in order for Heathcliff to solidify his claim on Thrushcross Grange. Heathcliff's actions clearly illustrate the philosophy that "the ends justify the means." In doing so, readers tend to root for Cathy to be able to somehow thwart Heathcliff's growing power. Nelly does not witness the wedding, but Cathy and Linton do indeed get married.

Glossary

enigmatical perplexing or baffling.

magnamity the ability to rise above pettiness or meanness.

ling heather.

vivisection medical research consisting of surgical operations or other experiments performed on living animals to study the structure and function of living organs and parts.

cockatrice deadly serpent in myth or the Bible.

Chapter 28

Summary

Zillah enters the bedroom on the fifth morning of Nelly's imprisonment, telling her that the village gossip has both Cathy and Nelly being lost in the marshes. Nelly finds Linton, who tells her that Cathy is being held prisoner and cannot be released. Unable to get Cathy free and unwilling to face Heathcliff, Nelly returns to the Grange.

She assures Edgar that Cathy is safe and will be home soon. She also dispatches servants to Wuthering Heights to bring Cathy home. The servants return empty-handed. Edgar sends for Mr. Green, a lawyer, to change his will. Nelly thinks she hears him arrive, but it is Cathy. With Linton's help, she has escaped.

Edgar and Cathy are reunited, and Edgar dies content, thinking his daughter is happily married. Later that evening, Mr. Green arrives and immediately takes charge of the Grange, dismissing all the servants except Nelly. He attempts to have Edgar buried in the chapel, but Nelly knows that Edgar's will clearly states that he is to be buried next to his wife. Cathy is permitted to stay at the Grange until after her father's burial.

Commentary

Nelly once again favors a lie instead of the truth, but this is probably advantageous for all involved, for nothing can be gained at this time by telling the truth to Edgar. Although Linton's words to Nelly echo his father's in regards to how he should treat his wife, Linton, in his own weakling way, finally stands up to his father when he enables Cathy to escape.

And Mr. Green symbolizes the extent of Heathcliff's interference, using money and influence to bend the laws, encouraging a lawyer to sacrifice one client for another. Heathcliff's retention of Nelly as housekeeper at Thrushcross Grange is his way of being practical, as well as rewarding her for showing what he considers to be loyalty.

Chapter 29

Summary

Heathcliff arrives to escort Cathy home, informing her that he punished Linton for his role in Cathy's escape. He refuses to allow Cathy to live at the Grange because he wants her to work for her keep, especially after Linton dies. Legally, both Linton and Heathcliff have greater claims to the Grange; thus, Cathy has no choice but to obey the directive of her father-in-law.

Cathy speaks out against Heathcliff, stating her love for Linton and that Heathcliff is alone in the world. As she is packing her things, Heathcliff confides in Nelly that he believes in ghosts, particularly the ghost of Catherine. Ever since her burial 18 years ago, he has been feeling her presence and seeing her. As he leaves, Heathcliff instructs Nelly not to visit Wuthering Heights, for she is not welcome.

Commentary

The fullest extent of Heathcliff's cruelty, what he does to Linton, is not shown on the page; rather, readers are able to leave it to their own imagination. Nonetheless, he makes it painfully clear that Linton will never cross him again.

Although he punishes his son, Heathcliff is not entirely without feelings. The loss of Catherine has tormented him, and oddly enough, after all Heathcliff has done to other characters, many readers again tend to sympathize with him for what he has endured. Brontë evokes this sympathy through Heathcliff's explanation that he has been disturbed nightly for 18 years, yearning to be reunited with Catherine yet having her just out of reach. Heathcliff's longing to be one with Catherine for eternity is the mark of a romantic, of a man truly in love and truly tormented by the loss of his love. Yet, true to his nature, he ends the chapter being as heartless as ever, informing Nelly that she is not to visit Wuthering Heights, effectively leaving Cathy alone in her new home.

Chapter 30

Summary

This chapter is the end of Nelly's narrative: Zillah now serves as Nelly's source of information about Cathy. Following Heathcliff's orders, Zillah refused to help Cathy when she first came to Wuthering Heights; Hareton was not able to do anything for her, either. Until the day Linton dies, Cathy tends to him herself. After his death, Cathy is not willing to let Zillah or Hareton be nice to her. At the end of the chapter, Lockwood, who is recuperated, informs Nelly that Heathcliff may look for another tenant for the Grange.

Commentary

The end of Nelly's primary narrative brings the story full circle to Chapter 1, when Lockwood first visited the Heights. Because of the cold reception she received after her father's death (per Heathcliff's instructions), Cathy is not friendly with either Zillah or Hareton; however, an attraction between Cathy and Hareton obviously exists: He offers her food and a seat by the fire, and she allows him to help her retrieve books that are out of reach. Neither one wants to admit having even a passing interest in the other, but both remember their friendly first meeting.

Heathcliff wants to prevent any friendship from developing between Hareton and Cathy because Hindley destroyed the relationship between Catherine and Heathcliff. Because he is miserable, he tries to ensure that no one else is happy.

Glossary

thrang busy.

hisseln himself.

farthing former small British coin equal to one fourth of a penny.

Chapter 31

Summary

Lockwood makes a trip to Wuthering Heights and carries a note from Nelly to Cathy. Hareton takes the note at first, but noticing Cathy's tears, returns it to her. She in turn still treats him coolly and makes fun of his attempts at reading. Embarrassed, Hareton flings his books into the fire.

When Heathcliff returns, he comments that Hareton favors Catherine more and more each day. This is something Heathcliff did not foresee and seems to disturb him. Now, in addition to the memories of his lost love, Heathcliff must also deal with Hareton's resemblance to his Aunt Catherine. Both the memories and physical reminder are beginning to take their toll on Heathcliff.

Commentary

Literary Device

This chapter provides foreshadowing for the end of the novel. Heathcliff is softening, and his plans for total revenge do not seem as important to him. Cathy and Hareton, although still arguing, show signs of developing a friendly relationship, and Lockwood, still the outsider, obviously must know more because he is the narrator of the events and they have not yet come to close.

Glossary

magpie a person who collects odds and ends.

Chevy Chase an old English ballad dealing with the Battle of Otterburn.

saturnine sluggish or morose.

Chapter 32

Summary

Six months later, Lockwood is in the area and returns to the Grange, only to find that Nelly is now living at Wuthering Heights. He travels there, and Nelly tells him what has happened since Lockwood left.

Two weeks after Lockwood departed from the Grange, Nelly was summoned to Wuthering Heights to be Cathy's companion because Zillah has left. While Nelly is there, Cathy admits to her that she was wrong to have made fun of Hareton, Hareton avoids Cathy, and Heathcliff withdraws from everyone.

After Hareton accidentally shoots himself and has to stay inside, he and Cathy argue but eventually make up and agree to be cousins. As a peace offering, Cathy wraps up a book and has Nelly present it to Hareton. If he accepts the book, Cathy will teach him to read and vows never to tease him again.

Commentary

A date, 1802, opens this chapter, calling to mind the first chapter and indicating the passage of time from whence Lockwood initially began his diary. As Lockwood returns to the area, he notices the disparity between the moors in winter and summer. Once again, the idea of a contrasting yet dual nature comes through. *Wuthering Heights* is based on contrasts, and as the novel nears its end, themes that were previously shown but not told are now being spoken of directly.

Literary Device

When Lockwood arrives at Wuthering Heights, he does not encounter a lock—the first sign that a change has taken place. The fragrance of flowers and fruit is the second. While Nelly mentions that Heathcliff has been dead for three months, she backs up in time to provide the details of the narrative that occurred between the time Lockwood left and his subsequent return.

In this chapter, forgiveness occurs for the first time. In a scene reminiscent of Catherine's death, Cathy begs forgiveness. This time, it is Hareton, not Heathcliff, who must decide, and he forgives her. With

Cathy and Hareton becoming allies, the second generation is not doomed to repeat the mistakes of the first. All that needs to fall into place is the death of Heathcliff.

Glossary

hostler a person who takes care of horses at an inn or stable.

glens narrow, secluded valleys.

heath a tract of open wasteland, especially in the British Isles, covered with heather and low shrubs; moor

fagots bundles of sticks and twigs.

fortnight a period of two weeks.

automatons persons or animals acting in an automatic or mechanical way.

morose ill-tempered, gloomy, or sullen.

beguiling passing (time) pleasantly.

obdurate stubborn.

Chapter 33

Summary

At breakfast the next morning, Hareton takes Cathy's side in an argument against Heathcliff. Heathcliff is about to strike her, but as he looks into Cathy's eyes, he controls himself. Later that night, he sees Hareton and Cathy sitting together. Cathy's eyes and Hareton's entire being remind him of Catherine. At this moment, Heathcliff admits to Nelly that he does not have the desire to complete his revenge. Everywhere at Wuthering Heights, Heathcliff is being constantly reminded of Catherine, and this is tormenting him.

Commentary

As Cathy and Hareton become friends, Heathcliff loses his desire for revenge. He refuses to speak of Cathy, but Hareton is the embodiment of Catherine and himself—her features and his personality come to life. The realities of this world are driving him mad, so Heathcliff seeks solitude more and more often.

Glossary

antipathy strong or deep-rooted dislike.

levers bars used for prying.

mattocks tools for loosening soil; a mattock is like a pickax but has a flat, adz-shaped blade.

monomania an excessive interest in or enthusiasm for some one thing.

laconic brief or terse in speech or expression.

Chapter 34

Summary

Heathcliff continues to seek solitude and only eats once a day. One night, a few days later, he leaves and is out all night. When he returns in the morning, Cathy remarks that he is actually quite pleasant. He rejects all food. When Nelly tries to encourage him to send for a minister, he scoffs at her and reminds her of his burial wishes. Later, Nelly sends for the doctor, but Heathcliff refuses to see him. The following night, Nelly finds Heathcliff's dead body. Hareton is the only one to mourn Heathcliff's dying. They bury Heathcliff according to his wishes, and villagers swear that he and another walk the moors.

Commentary

The growing love between Cathy and Hareton serves to intensify Heathcliff's loss. He, like Catherine, takes no food as he nears death. This is a ritual fasting. Food no longer sustains him; he needs to be nourished by something more. Heathcliff is consumed with pain as he longs to be united with Catherine.

Readers easily forgive, if not forget, what a monster Heathcliff had been, for he is such a pitiable shadow of his former self. *Wuthering Heights* ends on a universal note, with love conquering hate.

Glossary

admonition a mild rebuke; reprimand.

fender a low screen in front of a fireplace to keep hot coals in.

Titan any person or thing of great size or power.

caper a gay, playful jump or leap.

levity lack of seriousness.

sovereign a British gold coin valued at twenty shillings or one pound sterling, no longer minted for circulation.

CHARACTER ANALYSES

The following critical analyses delve into the physical, emotional, and psychological traits of the literary work's major characters so that you might better understand what motivates these characters. The writer of this study guide provides this scholarship as an educational tool by which you may compare your own interpretations of the characters. Before reading the character analyses that follow, consider first writing your own short essays on the characters as an exercise by which you can test your understanding of the original literary work. Then, compare your essays to those that follow, noting discrepancies between the two. If your essays appear lacking, that might indicate that you need to re-read the original literary work or re-familiarize yourself with the major characters.

Heathcliff

To everyone but Catherine Hareton, Heathcliff seems to be an inhuman monster—or even incarnate evil. From a literary perspective, he is more the embodiment of the Byronic hero (attributed to the writer George Gordon, Lord Byron), a man of stormy emotions who shuns humanity because he himself has been ostracized; a rebellious hero who functions as a law unto himself. Heathcliff is both despicable and pitiable. His one sole passion is Catherine, yet his commitment to his notion of a higher love does not seem to include forgiveness.

Readers need to determine if his revenge is focused on his lost position at Wuthering Heights, his loss of Catherine to Edgar, or if it his assertion of dignity as a human being. The difficulty most readers have relating to and understanding Heathcliff is the fact that he hates as deeply as he loves; therefore, he is despised as much as he is pitied.

Catherine Earnshaw

Often viewed as the epitome of the free spirit, Catherine is torn between two worlds. On one hand, she longs to be with Heathcliff, her soul mate: their life together, growing up and playing on the moors, represents the freedom and innocence of childhood. On the other, she recognizes what a marriage to Edgar can do for her socially, and she enjoys those things that Edgar can provide for her. Ultimately, she is self-absorbed and self-centered, and although she claims to love both Heathcliff and Edgar, she loves herself more, and this selfish love ends up hurting everyone who cares for her.

Not until she nears death does Catherine turn exclusively towards Heathcliff, abandoning Edgar. Ironically, Heathcliff does not fully forgive her, and because of this, Edgar is the man who gives every appearance of loving Catherine unconditionally.

Edgar Linton

Edgar represents the typical Victorian hero, possessing qualities of constancy and tenderness; however, a non-emotional intellectual is not the type of person who can make Catherine happy in the long run. Edgar loves and understands Catherine more than anyone realizes, but love alone is not enough to sustain a relationship. He ends up losing everything—his wife, his sister, his daughter, and his home—to Heathcliff because good does not always overcome evil. He is a foil for Heathcliff.

Cathy Linton

Cathy's nature, a combination of both her parents, is key to revising the past. Her wildness and willfulness lead her to Wuthering Heights and the problems and pitfalls related therein. Her constant loyalty, good nature, and perseverance, however, eventually restore order and love to the farmhouse, thwarting Heathcliff's plans for revenge.

Just as Catherine's presence dominates the first half of the text, Cathy's rules the second. Edgar tries to keep her from Wuthering Heights (and from Heathcliff), but her attraction to a man and her independent nature—characteristics that mirror her mother—once again make Edgar's appeals ineffective.

Hareton Earnshaw

More of a son to Heathcliff than Linton, Hareton exhibits a sense of nobility by remaining loyal to the only father he ever really knew. Although he loses his inheritance, he does not bear a grudge toward Heathcliff. For most of the text, he serves as a reminder to Heathcliff of what his father, Hindley, had done. But toward the end of the novel, Hareton begins to remind Heathcliff of Catherine. Hareton even stands up to Heathcliff on Cathy's behalf.

Because he has never experienced love himself, readers do not know for sure of Hareton's capacity for it; however, his pairing with Cathy at the end of *Wuthering Heights* seems to suggest what Heathcliff may have been like under different circumstances.

Ellen (Nelly) Dean

Nelly serves as both outsider and insider as she narrates the primary story of *Wuthering Heights*. Although she does not exhibit the extreme lengths of cruelty shown by Heathcliff and Catherine, Nelly often is an instigator who enjoys the conflict around her. Nelly can be seen as a combination of Heathcliff's cruelty and Catherine's self-centeredness.

CRITICAL ESSAYS

On the pages that follow, the writer of this study guide provides critical scholarship on various aspects of Emily Bronte's *Wuthering Heights.* These interpretive essays are intended solely to enhance your understanding of the original literary work; they are supplemental materials and are not to replace your reading of *Wuthering Heights.* When you're finished reading *Wuthering Heights,* and prior to your reading this study guide's critical essays, consider making a bulleted list of what you think are the most important themes and symbols. Write a short paragraph under each bullet explaining *why* you think that theme or symbol is important; include at least one short quote from the original literary work that supports your contention. Then, test your list and reasons against those found in the following essays. Do you include themes and symbols that the study guide author doesn't? If so, this self test might indicate that you are well on your way to understanding original literary work. But if not, perhaps you will need to re-read *Wuthering Heights.*

The Narrative Structure

Although Lockwood and Nelly serve as the obvious narrators, others are interspersed throughout the novel—Heathcliff, Isabella, Cathy, even Zillah—who narrate a chapter or two, providing insight into both character and plot development. Catherine does not speak directly to the readers (except in quoted dialogue), but through her diary, she narrates important aspects of the childhood she and Heathcliff shared on the moors and the treatment they received at the hands of Joseph and Hindley. All of the voices weave together to provide a choral narrative. Initially, they speak to Lockwood, answering his inquiries, but they speak to readers, also, providing multiple views of the tangled lives of the inhabitants of Thrushcross Grange and Wuthering Heights.

Brontë appears to present objective observers, in an attempt to allow the story to speak for itself. Objective observations by outsiders would presumably not be tainted by having a direct involvement; unfortunately, a closer examination of these two seemingly objective narrators reveals their bias.

For example, Lockwood's narrative enables readers to begin the story when most of the action is already completed. Although the main story is being told in flashback, having Lockwood interact with Heathcliff and the others at Wuthering Heights immediately displaces his objectivity. What he records in his diary is not just what he is being told by Nelly but his memories and interpretation of Nelly's tale. Likewise, Nelly's narrative directly involves the reader and engages them in the action. While reporting the past, she is able to foreshadow future events, which builds suspense, thereby engaging readers even more. But her involvement is problematic because she is hypocritical in her actions: sometimes choosing Edgar over Heathcliff (and vice versa), and at times working with Cathy while at other times betraying Cathy's confidence. Nonetheless, she is quite an engaging storyteller, so readers readily forgive her shortcomings.

Ultimately, both Lockwood and Nelly are merely facilitators, enabling readers to enter the world of *Wuthering Heights*. All readers know more than any one narrator, and therefore are empowered as they read.

Class Structure

In the Victorian Era, social class was not solely dependent upon the amount of money a person had; rather, the source of income, birth, and family connections played a major role in determining one's position in society. And, significantly, most people accepted their place in the hierarchy. In addition to money, manners, speech, clothing, education, and values revealed a person's class. The three main classes were the elite class, the middle class, and the working class. Further divisions existed within these three class distinctions.

The characters in *Wuthering Heights* demonstrate the nature of this class-structured society. The Lintons were the most elite family in the novel, and Thrushcross Grange was a superior property to Wuthering Heights, yet they were not members of the uppercrust of society; rather, they were the professional middle class.

Although Wuthering Heights was a farmhouse, the Earnshaws were not members of the working class because they were landowners who had servants. Their station in society was below the Lintons but not significantly below. Nelly, a servant of the Earnshaws, represents the lower middle class—those who worked non-manual labor. Servants were superior to manual laborers, which explains the problems created by Heathcliff.

Heathcliff is an orphan; therefore, his station is below everyone else in *Wuthering Heights*. It was unheard of to raise someone from the working class as a member of the middle-to-upper middle class. Even Nelly, who was raised with the Earnshaw children, understood her place below her childhood friends. When Mr. Earnshaw elevates the status of Heathcliff, eventually favoring him to his own son, this goes against societal norms.

This combination of elevation and usurpation is why Hindley returns Heathcliff to his previous low station after the death of Mr. Earnshaw, and that is why Heathcliff relishes in the fact that Hindley's son Hareton is reduced to the level of a common, uneducated laborer. And social class must be the reason Catherine marries Edgar; she is attracted to the social comforts he can supply her. No other plausible explanation exists. Catherine naively thinks she can marry Edgar and then use her position and his money to assist Heathcliff, but that would never happen.

When Heathcliff returns, having money is not enough for Edgar to consider him a part of acceptable society. Heathcliff uses his role as the outcast to encourage Isabella's infatuation. The feelings that both Catherine and Isabella have for Heathcliff, the common laborer, cause them to lose favor with their brothers. Hindley and Edgar cannot accept the choices their sisters make and therefore, withdraw their love. When a woman betrays her class, she is betraying her family and her class—both unacceptable actions.

Major Themes

Of the major themes in *Wuthering Heights*, the nature of love—both romantic and brotherly but, oddly enough, not erotic—applies to the principal characters as well as the minor ones. Every relationship in the text is strained at one point or another. Brontë's exploration of love is best discussed in the context of good versus evil (which is another way of saying love versus hate). Although the polarities between good and evil are easily understood, the differences are not that easily applied to the characters and their actions.

The most important relationship is the one between Heathcliff and Catherine. The nature of their love seems to go beyond the kind of love most people know. In fact, it is as if their love is beyond this world, belonging on a spiritual plane that supercedes anything available to everyone else on Earth. Their love seems to be born out of their rebellion and not merely a sexual desire. They both, however, do not fully understand the nature of their love, for they betray one another: Each of them marry a person whom they know they do not love as much as they love each other.

Contrasting the capacity for love is the ability to hate. And Heathcliff hates with a vengeance. Heathcliff initially focuses his hate toward Hindley, then to Edgar, and then to a certain extent, to Catherine. Because of his hate, Heathcliff resorts to what is another major theme in *Wuthering Heights*—revenge. Hate and revenge intertwine with selfishness to reveal the conflicting emotions that drive people to do things that are not particularly nice or rationale. Some choices are regretted while others are relished.

These emotions make the majority of the characters in *Wuthering Heights* well rounded and more than just traditional stereotypes. Instead of symbolizing a particular emotion, characters symbolize real people with real, oftentimes not-so-nice emotions. Every character has at least one redeeming trait or action with which the reader can empathize. This empathy is a result of the complex nature of the characters and results in a depiction of life in the Victorian Era, a time when people behaved very similarly to the way they do today.

Heathcliff's Obsession

Throughout *Wuthering Heights* two distinct yet related obsessions drive Heathcliff's character: his desire for Catherine's love and his need for revenge. Catherine, the object of his obsession, becomes the essence of his life, yet, in a sense, he ends up murdering his love. Ironically, after her death, Heathcliff's obsession only intensifies.

Heathcliff's love for Catherine enables him to endure Hindley's maltreatment after Mr. Earnshaw's death. But after overhearing Catherine admit that she could not marry him, Heathcliff leaves. Nothing is known of his life away from her, but he returns with money. Heathcliff makes an attempt to join the society to which Catherine is drawn. Upon his return, she favors him to Edgar but still he cannot have her. He is constantly present, lurking around Thrushcross Grange, visiting after hours, and longing to be buried in a connected grave with her so their bodies would disintegrate into one. Ironically, his obsession with revenge seemingly outweighs his obsession with his love, and that is why he does not fully forgive Catherine for marrying Edgar.

After Catherine's death, he must continue his revenge—a revenge that starts as Heathcliff assumes control of Hindley's house and his son—and continues with Heathcliff taking everything that is Edgar's. Although Heathcliff constantly professes his love for Catherine, he has no problem attempting to ruin the life of her daughter. He views an ambiguous world as black and white: a world of haves and have-nots. And for too long, he has been the outsider. That is why he is determined to take everything away from those at Wuthering Heights and Thrushcross Grange who did not accept him. For Heathcliff, revenge is a more powerful emotion than love.

CliffsNotes Review

Use this CliffsNotes Review to test your understanding of the original text, and reinforce what you've learned in this book. After you work through the essay questions and useful practice projects, you're well on your way to understanding a comprehensive and meaningful interpretation of *Wuthering Heights*.

Q&A

1. Heathcliff and Catherine grew up together playing on the _____.

2. Although Catherine loves Heathcliff, she marries _____.

3. After her marriage, Catherine leaves Wuthering Heights to live at _____.

4. Heathcliff forces Cathy to marry _____.

5. At the end of the novel, Cathy is going to marry _____.

Answers: (1) moors. (2) Edgar. (3) Thrushcross Grange. (4) Linton. (5) Hareton.

Identify the Quote: Find Each Quote in *Wuthering Heights*

1. "Come in! come in!" he sobbed. "Cathy, do come. Oh, do—*once* more!"

2. "It would degrade me to marry Heathcliff now; so he shall never know how I love him; and that, not because he's handsome, Nelly, but because he's more myself than I am. Whatever our souls are made of, his and mine are the same."

3. "My love for Linton is like the foliage in the woods . . . My love for Heathcliff resembles the eternal rocks beneath."

4. "It is impossible for you to be *my* friend and *his* at the same time; and I absolutely *require* to know which you choose."

5. "I'll not lie there by myself; they may bury me twelve feet deep, and throw the church down over me, but I won't rest till you are with me. I never will!"

6. "I have not broken your heart—*you* have broken it—and in breaking it, you have broken mine."

7. " . . . take any form—drive me mad! only *do* not leave me in this abyss, where I cannot find you! Oh God! it is unutterable! I *cannot* live without my life! I *cannot* live without my soul!"

8. "Despise me as much as you please; I am a worthless, cowardly wretch—I can't be scorned enough! but I'm too mean for your anger—hate my father, spare me, for contempt!"

9. " . . . *you* have *nobody* to love you; and, however miserable you make us, we shall still have the revenge of thinking that your cruelty rises from your greater misery! You *are* miserable, are you not? Lonely, like the devil, and envious like him? *Nobody* loves you—*nobody* will cry for you, when you die! I wouldn't be you!"

10. " . . . she has disturbed me, night and day, through eighteen years—incessantly—remorselessly—til yesternight; and yesternight, I was tranquil. I dreamt I was sleeping the last sleep, by that sleeper, with my heart stopped, and my cheek frozen against hers."

Answers: (1) Heathcliff to Catherine's ghost, out the window in the room where Lockwood was spending the night. (2) Catherine to Nelly and overheard by Heathcliff. (3) Catherine to Nelly, explaining the nature of her love .(4) Edgar to Catherine, forcing her to choose between Heathcliff and himself. (5) Catherine (in a delirious state) to Heathcliff (6) Heathcliff to Catherine, while she is on her deathbed, begging him to forgive her. (7) Heathcliff to Catherine's spirit (8) Linton to Cathy, after she is tricked into entering Wuthering Heights. (9) Cathy to Heathcliff, when he arrives to escort her from Thrushcross Grange to Wuthering Heights. (10) Heathcliff to Nelly, about resting peacefully for the first time in years.

Essay Questions

1. Is *Wuthering Heights* a novel about love? If so, what kind? If not, what is its primary theme?

2. Although Nelly and Lockwood are the primary narrators, other characters get to narrate a chapter or two, though Edgar does not. What effect does the lack of insight into his character's point of view have on *Wuthering Heights*?

3. Compare and contrast Wuthering Heights and Thrushcross Grange.

4. What role does the supernatural play in *Wuthering Heights*?

5. A multitude of ordered pairs exist throughout the text. What are the most significant dualities? What does Brontë gain by creating symmetry between generations? What does she lose?

Practice Project

Create a *Wuthering Heights* Web page that is linked to your school's Web site. This Web-page project should serve as the culminating activity that acts as a review and furthers your knowledge and understanding of the novel. This project has three major steps:

1. Choose the content of the page.

Determine which major topics you want to address. Some suggestions include themes, characters, plot, and imagery. In addition to the literary aspects of *Wuthering Heights*, consider including information that will enhance a reader's understanding and appreciation of the text.

2. Use a variety of search engines to find appropriate links.

3. Design your page.

When planning the layout, consider ease of use as well as how it looks. A well-designed page will provide others the opportunity to share in your learning.

CliffsNotes Resource Center

The learning doesn't need to stop here. CliffsNotes Resource Center shows you the best of the best—links to the best information in print and online about the author and/or related works. And don't think that this is all we've prepared for you; we've put all kinds of pertinent information at www.cliffsnotes.com. Look for all the terrific resources at your favorite bookstore or local library and on the Internet. When you're online, make your first stop www.cliffsnotes.com where you'll find more incredibly useful information about *Wuthering Heights*.

Books and Periodicals

This CliffsNotes book, published by Wiley Publishing, Inc., provides a meaningful interpretation of *Wuthering Heights*. If you are looking for information about the author and/or related works, check out these other publications:

MARSH, NICHOLAS. *Emily Brontë: Wuthering Heights (Analysing Texts)*. New York: St. Martin's Press, 1999. This contemporary analysis serves as an introduction to the characters, symbols, and imagery used throughout *Wuthering Heights*.

COLE, DAVID W. "'The Fate of Milo' and the Moral Vision of *Wuthering Heights*." *ANQ* 11 (Spring 98): 23–29. Cole addresses the moral consequences of character and conduct as they pertain to *Wuthering Heights*, particularly through the main character Catherine.

GALEF, DAVID. "Keeping One's Distance: Irony and Doubling in *Wuthering Heights*." *Studies in the Novel* 24 (Fall 92): 242–249. Galef shows the pattern between characters throughout the novel and focuses specifically on Lockwood and Isabella.

TYLER, LISA. "Passion and Grief in *A Farewell to Arms*: Ernest Hemingway's Retelling of *Wuthering Heights*." *Hemingway Review* 14 (Spring 95): 79–97. Tyler provides evidence of potential influences that Brontë's novel may have had on *A Farewell to Arms*, stressing strong similarities in theme and style.

It's easy to find books published by Wiley Publishing, Inc. and other publishers. You'll find them in your favorite bookstores (on the Internet and at a store near you). We also have three Web sites that you can use to read about all the books we publish:

- www.cliffsnotes.com

- www.dummies.com

- www.wiley.com

Films and Audio

Wuthering Heights. Dir. William Wyler. With Laurence Olivier and Merle Oberon. A Samuel Goldwyn Company Production, distributed by Embassy Home Entertainment, 1939. Although this version only concerns itself with the first half of the novel, it is still considered the best adaptation.

Wuthering Heights. (8 cassettes, unabridged.) Blackstone Audio Books, 1992. Although abridgments are available, the best way to experience Brontë's novel is listening to the entire text. For those who do not like to read, narrator Nadia May provides a pleasant voice.

Internet

Check out these Web resources for more information about *Wuthering Heights* and Emily Brontë:

About.com, http://classiclit.about.com—serves as a starting point for personal information about Brontë, international links, and overview of themes and techniques.

The Victorian Literature Web site, http://victorian. fortunecity.com/whistler/23/index.html—provides biographical, textual, and historical information about Brontë and her contemporaries.

Next time you're on the Internet, don't forget to drop by www.cliffs notes.com. We've created an online Resource Center that you can use today, tomorrow, and beyond.

Appendix: Genealogy

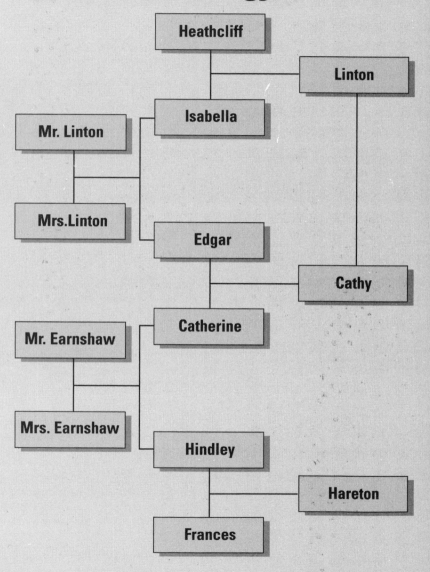

Index

The Odyssey
Oedipus Trilogy
Of Human Bondage
Of Mice and Men
The Old Man and
the Sea
Old Testament
Oliver Twist
The Once and
Future King
One Day in the Life of
Ivan Denisovich
One Flew Over
Cuckoo's Nest
100 Years of Solitude
O'Neill's Plays
Othello
Our Town
The Outsiders
The Ox Bow Incident
Paradise Lost
A Passage to India
The Pearl
The Pickwick Papers
The Picture of
Dorian Gray
Pilgrim's Progress
The Plague
Plato's Euthyphro…
Plato's The Republic
Poe's Short Stories
A Portrait of the
Artist…
The Portrait of a Lady
The Power and
the Glory
Pride and Prejudice
The Prince
The Prince and
the Pauper
A Raisin in the Sun
The Red Badge of
Courage
The Red Pony
The Return of the
Native
Richard II
Richard III

The Rise of
Silas Lapham
Robinson Crusoe
Roman Classics
Romeo and Juliet
The Scarlet Letter
A Separate Peace
Shakespeare's
Comedies
Shakespeare's Histories
Shakespeare's
Minor Plays
Shakespeare's Sonnets
Shakespeare's Tragedies
Shaw's Pygmalion &
Arms…
Silas Marner
Sir Gawain…Green
Knight
Sister Carrie
Slaughterhouse-Five
Snow Falling on Cedars
Song of Solomon
Sons and Lovers
The Sound and the Fury
Steppenwolf &
Siddhartha
The Stranger
The Sun Also Rises
T.S. Eliot's Poems &
Plays
A Tale of Two Cities
The Taming of the
Shrew
Tartuffe, Misanthrope…
The Tempest
Tender Is the Night
Tess of the D'Urbervilles
Their Eyes Were
Watching God
Things Fall Apart
The Three Musketeers
To Kill a Mockingbird
Tom Jones
Tom Sawyer
Treasure Island &
Kidnapped
The Trial

Tristram Shandy
Troilus and Cressida
Twelfth Night
Ulysses
Uncle Tom's Cabin
The Unvanquished
Utopia
Vanity Fair
Vonnegut's Works
Waiting for Godot
Walden
Walden Two
War and Peace
Who's Afraid of
Virginia…
Winesburg, Ohio
The Winter's Tale
The Woman Warrior
Worldly Philosophers
Wuthering Heights
A Yellow Raft in
Blue Water

Check Out the All-New CliffsNotes Guides

TECHNOLOGY TOPICS

Balancing Your Check-
book with Quicken
Buying and Selling
on eBay
Buying Your First PC
Creating a Winning
PowerPoint 2000
Presentation
Creating Web Pages
with HTML
Creating Your First
Web Page
Exploring the World
with Yahoo!
Getting on the Internet
Going Online with AOL
Making Windows 98
Work for You

Setting Up a
Windows 98
Home Network
Shopping Online Safely
Upgrading and
Repairing Your PC
Using Your First iMac
Using Your First PC
Writing Your First
Computer Program

PERSONAL FINANCE TOPICS

Budgeting & Saving
Your Money
Getting a Loan
Getting Out of Debt
Investing for the
First Time
Investing in
401(k) Plans
Investing in IRAs
Investing in
Mutual Funds
Investing in the
Stock Market
Managing Your Money
Planning Your
Retirement
Understanding
Health Insurance
Understanding
Life Insurance

CAREER TOPICS

Delivering a Winning
Job Interview
Finding a Job
on the Web
Getting a Job
Writing a Great Resume